SMASHING
Professional
Web Design

THE BEST OF SMASHING MAGAZINE

SMASHING
Professional
Web Design

THE BEST OF SMASHING MAGAZINE

Smashing Magazine

A John Wiley and Sons, Ltd, Publication

This edition first published 2011
© 2011 Smashing Media GmbH

Registered office
John Wiley & Sons Ltd, The Atrium, Southern Gate, Chichester, West Sussex,
PO19 8SQ, United Kingdom

A catalogue record for this book is available from the British Library.

978-1-119-99275-2

Set in 9.5/11.5 Minion Pro by Wiley Composition Services
Printed in the U.S. by CJK

PUBLISHER'S ACKNOWLEDGEMENTS

Some of the people who helped bring this book to market include the following:

Editorial and Production
VP Consumer and Technology Publishing Director: Michelle Leete
Associate Director–Book Content Management: Martin Tribe
Associate Publisher: Chris Webb
Publishing Assistant: Ellie Scott
Senior Project Editor: Sara Shlaer
Editorial Manager: Jodi Jensen
Editorial Assistant: Leslie Saxman
Proofreader: Andrew Lobo

Marketing
Senior Marketing Manager: Louise Breinholt
Marketing Executive: Kate Parrett

Composition Services
Compositor: Wiley Indianapolis Composition Services
Proofreader: Linda Seifert
Indexer: Potomac Indexing, LLC

Cover design input from Andrea Austoni,
cutelittlefactory.com

Contents

CONTENTS

xi

CONTENTS

x

Preface

Smashing Magazine has grown a lot over the last years. We worked very hard to turn a small blog into a professional online publication with in-depth articles written by professionals and carefully prepared and edited by our team. We are fully aware of the responsibility we have in the community, and we are doing our best to promote best practices and help designers out there to get a better understanding of professionalism in our industry.

This book is one of our humble attempts to support the design community by providing professional and valuable advice, professional tips and practical insights. The book contains a selection of the best articles about professional Web design that were published on Smashing Magazine in 2009 and 2010. The articles have been carefully edited and prepared for the printed edition.

This book presents guidelines for professional Web development, including communicating with clients, creating a road map to a successful portfolio, rules for professional networking, and tips on designing user interfaces for business Web applications. The book also shares expert advice for students and young Web designers, and it also helps you learn how to respond effectively to design criticism, use storytelling for a better user experience, and apply color theory to your professional designs.

Please let us know what you think of the book in your reviews and comments. And thank you for your trust and your support over all these years — it means a world to us.

-- Vitaly Friedman, Sven Lennartz, and the Team

1

HARSH TRUTHS ABOUT CORPORATE WEBSITES

By Paul Boag

WE ALL MAKE mistakes running our websites. However, the nature of those mistakes varies depending on the size of your company. As your organization grows, the mistakes change. This article addresses common mistakes made by large organizations.

Most of the clients I work with are large organizations: universities, large charities, public sector institutions, and big companies. Over the last seven years, I have noticed certain recurring misconceptions among these organizations. This article aims to dispel these illusions and encourage people to face the harsh reality.

The problem is that if you are reading this, you are probably already aware of these things. But hopefully this article will be helpful to you as you convince others within your organization. In any case, here are some of the *harsh truths about websites of large organizations*.

YOU NEED A SEPARATE WEB DIVISION

In many organizations, the website is managed by either the marketing or IT department. However, this inevitably leads to a turf war, with the website becoming the victim of internal politics.

In reality, pursuing a Web strategy is not particularly suited to either group. IT may be excellent at rolling out complex systems, but it is not suited to developing a friendly user experience or establishing an online brand.

Marketing, on the other hand, is little better. As Jeffrey Zeldman puts it in his article "Let There Be Web Divisions:"

> *The Web is a conversation. Marketing, by contrast, is a mono-logue… And then there's all that messy business with semantic markup, CSS, unobtrusive scripting, card-sorting exercises, HTML run-throughs, involving users in accessibility, and the rest of the skills and experience that don't fall under Marketing's purview.*

Jeffrey Zeldman urges organizations to create a separate Web division.

Copyright © 1995–2010 L. Jeffrey Zeldman.

Instead, the website should be managed by a single unified team. Again, Zeldman sums it up when he writes:

> *Put them in a division that recognizes that your website is not a bastard of your brochures, nor a natural outgrowth of your group calendar. Let there be Web divisions.*
> http://www.zeldman.com/2007/07/02/let-there-be-web-divisions/

MANAGING YOUR WEBSITE IS A FULL-TIME JOB

Not only is the website often split between marketing and IT, it is also usually under-resourced. Instead of there being a dedicated Web team, those responsible for the website are often expected to run it alongside their "day job." When a Web team is in place, it is often over-stretched. The vast majority of its time is spent on day-to-day maintenance rather than on longer-term strategic thinking.

This situation is further aggravated by the fact that the people hired to "maintain" the website are typically junior members of the staff. They do not have the experience or authority to push the website forward. It is time for organizations to seriously invest in their websites and finally move their Web strategies forward by hiring full-time senior Web managers.

PERIODIC REDESIGN IS NOT ENOUGH

Because corporate websites are under-resourced, they are often neglected for long periods of time. They slowly become out of date in their content, design, and technology. Eventually, the website becomes such an embarrassment that management steps in and demands that it be sorted. This inevitably leads to a complete redesign at considerable expense. This is a flawed approach. It is a waste of money, because when the old website is replaced, the investment that was put into it is lost, too. It is also tough on finances, with a large expenditure having to be made every few years.

Cameron Moll encourages Web designers to realign, not redesign.

A better way is continual investment in your website, allowing it to evolve over time. Not only is this less wasteful, it is also better for users, as pointed out by Cameron Moll in his post "Good Designers Redesign, Great Designers Realign" (http://www.alistapart.com/articles/redesignrealign).

YOUR WEBSITE CANNOT APPEAL TO EVERYONE

One of the first questions I ask a client is, "Who is your target audience?" I am regularly shocked at the length of the reply. Too often, it includes a long and detailed list of diverse people. Inevitably, my next question is, "Which of those many demographic groups are most important?" Depressingly, the answer is usually that they are all equally important.

The harsh truth is that if you build a website for everyone, it will appeal to no one. It is important to be extremely focused about your audience and cater your design and content to it. Does this mean you should ignore your other users? Not at all. Your website should be accessible by all and not offend or exclude anybody. However, the website does need to be primarily aimed at a clearly defined audience.

YOU ARE WASTING MONEY ON SOCIAL NETWORKING

I find it encouraging that website managers increasingly recognize that a Web strategy involves more than running a website. They are beginning to use tools such as Twitter, Facebook, and YouTube to increase their reach and engage with new audiences. However, although they are using these tools, too often they do so ineffectively. Tweeting on a corporate account or posting sales demonstrations on YouTube misses the essence of social networking.

Social networking is about people engaging with people. Individuals do not want to build relationships with brands and corporations. They want to talk to other people. Too many organizations throw millions into Facebook apps and viral videos when they could spend that money on engaging with people in a transparent and open way.

Instead of creating a corporate Twitter account or indeed even a corporate blog, encourage your employees to start tweeting and blogging themselves. Provide guidelines on acceptable behavior and what tools they need to start engaging directly with the community that is connected to your products and services. This demonstrates your commitment not only to the community but also to the human side of your business.

Microsoft dramatically improved its image among the development community by allowing staff to speak out via the Channel 9 website.

YOUR WEBSITE IS NOT ALL ABOUT YOU

While some website managers want their website to appeal to everyone, others want it to appeal to themselves and their colleagues. A surprising number of organizations ignore their users entirely and base their websites entirely on an organizational perspective. This typically manifests itself in inappropriate design that caters to the managing director's personal preferences and in content that is full of jargon.

A website should not pander to the preferences of staff but should rather meet the needs of its users. Too many designs are rejected because the boss "doesn't like green." Likewise, too much website copy contains acronyms and terms used only within the organization.

YOU'RE NOT GETTING VALUE FROM YOUR WEB TEAM

Whether they have an in-house Web team or use an external agency, many organizations fail to get the most from their Web designers. Web designers are much more than pixel pushers. They have a wealth of knowledge about the Web and how users interact with it. They also understand design techniques, including grid systems, white space, color theory, and much more.

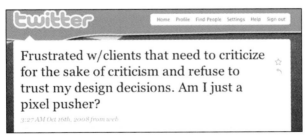

Treating designers as pixel pushers wastes their experience: here, a designer laments his predicament on Twitter.

It is therefore wasteful to micro-manage by asking them to "make the logo bigger" or to "move that element three pixels to the left." By doing so, you are reducing their role to that of a software operator and are wasting the wealth of experience they bring.

If you want to get the maximum return on your Web team, present it with problems, not solutions. For example, if you're targeting your website at teenage girls, and the designer goes for corporate blue, suggest that your audience might not respond well to that color. Do not tell him or her to change it to pink. This way, the designer has the freedom to find a solution that may be even better than your choice. You're allowing your designer to solve the problem you have presented.

DESIGN BY COMMITTEE BRINGS DEATH

The ultimate symbol of a large organization's approach to website management is the committee. A committee is often formed to tackle the website because internal politics demand that everyone have a say and that all considerations be taken into account.

To say that all committees are a bad idea is naive, and to suggest that a large corporate website could be developed without consultation is fanciful. But when it comes to design, committees are often the kiss of death.

Design is subjective. The way we respond to a design is influenced by culture, gender, age, childhood experience, and even physical conditions (such as color blindness). What one person considers great design could be hated by another. This is why it is so important that design decisions be informed by user testing rather than personal experience. Unfortunately, this approach is rarely taken when a committee is making the decisions.

Instead, designing by committee becomes about compromise. Because committee members have different opinions about the design, they look for common ground. One person hates the blue color scheme, while another loves it. This leads to designing on the fly, with the committee instructing the designer to "try a different blue" in the hopes of finding middle ground. Unfortunately, this leads only to bland design that neither appeals to nor excites anyone.

A CMS IS NOT A SILVER BULLET

Many of the clients I work with have amazingly unrealistic expectations of content management systems (CMS). Those without one think it will solve all of their content woes, and those who have one moan because it hasn't!

It is certainly true that a CMS can bring a lot of benefits. These include:

- Reducing the technical barriers of adding content
- Allowing more people to add and edit content
- Facilitating faster updates
- Allowing greater control

But many CMS's are less flexible than their owners would like. They fail to meet the changing demands of the websites they are a platform for. Website managers also complain that their CMS is hard to use. In many cases, this is because the ones using it have not been adequately trained or are not using it regularly enough.

Finally, a CMS may allow content to be easily updated, but it does not ensure that content will be updated or even that the quality of content will be acceptable. Many CMS-based websites still have out-of-date content or poorly written copy. This is because internal processes have not been put in place to support the content contributors.

If you look to a CMS to solve your website maintenance issues, you will be disappointed.

YOU HAVE TOO MUCH CONTENT

Part of the problem with maintaining content on large corporate websites is that there is too much content in the first place. Most of these websites have "evolved" over years, with more and more content being added. At no point did anyone review the content and ask what could be taken away.

Many website managers fill their website with copy that nobody will read. This happens because of one or more of the following:

- A fear of missing something: by putting everything online, they believe users will be able to find whatever they want. Unfortunately, with so much information available, it is hard to find anything.
- A fear that users will not understand: whether from a lack of confidence in their website or in their audience, they feel the need to provide endless instruction to users. Unfortunately, users never read this copy.
- A desperate desire to convince: they are desperate to sell their product or communicate their message, and so they bloat the text with sales copy that actually conveys little valuable information.

Steve Krug, in his book *Don't Make Me Think,* encourages website managers to "get rid of half the words on each page, then get rid of half of what's left." This will reduce the noise level on each page and make the useful content more prominent.

CONCLUSIONS

Large organizations do a lot right in running their websites. However, they also face some unique challenges that can lead to painful mistakes. Resolving these problems means accepting that mistakes have been made, overcoming internal politics, and changing the way they control their brand. Doing this will give you a significant competitive advantage and make your Web strategy more effective over the long term.

Paul Boag is the founder of UK Web design agency Headscape, author of the Website Owner's Manual, *and host of the award-winning Web design podcast Boagworld.*

2

PORTFOLIO DESIGN STUDY: DESIGN PATTERNS AND CURRENT PRACTICES

By Vitaly Friedman

FOLLOWING THE REQUESTS of our readers on Smashing Magazine, we have carefully selected dozens of design and Web development agencies, analyzed their portfolio websites, and identified popular design patterns. The main goal of the study was to provide freelancers and design agencies with useful pointers for designing their own portfolio.

We have brainstormed on the most important design issues and asked designers across the globe what decisions they often have to make when designing a portfolio website. We also asked designers what questions they would like answered or analyzed in our case study.

In the end, we came up with a bag of 40 solid portfolio-related questions — sorted, grouped, and ranked according to importance. We searched for a good mix of established design agencies and well-designed portfolio websites of small and large agencies.

Finally, we created a questionnaire of 40 questions and went through the websites of all of these design agencies, noticing design patterns and filling out our quite lengthy forms. Overall, the study took over 75 hours to prepare.

This article presents the initial results of our big portfolio design study. In the following pages, we discuss the visual design, structure, layout, and navigation of portfolio websites. We also get into the design details of every single page, including the About, Clients, Services, Portfolio, Workflow, and Contact pages. Of course, you do not necessarily have to follow the findings presented here; rather, get from them a general idea of what other portfolios look like, and then come up with something of your own that is usable, distinctive, and memorable. We thank Mark Nutter for helping us gather data for this study.

LIGHT VS. DARK DESIGN

A general question that comes up often is whether to design a visually appealing dark website (that is, use big bold typography and vivid colors to give the user a colorful and memorable experience) or a softer lighter website (one that has a simple structure and clean typography).

Surprisingly, according to our studies:

- 82% of portfolio websites have a light design with neutral calm colors. The backgrounds of these websites are generally a light shade of gray or yellow, rather than pure white.
- 29% of portfolio websites have vibrant, striking colors.
- Dark websites are much more likely to have big typography and strong visuals.

Of course, picking a dark or light design depends strongly on your personal approach and individual goals for the portfolio. Saying that the "trend" strongly favors light designs would be inaccurate because each type serves its purpose in its particular context.

HOW MANY COLUMNS?

Interestingly, many of the portfolio websites we researched tend to vary the number of columns between sections. Client and About pages usually have two columns, while front pages often have three to four columns and present the most important sections of the website in a compact overview. In fact, we see pages getting more and more columns: every sixth portfolio website we saw has at least one page with four columns.

According to our study, few websites risk experimenting with so-called out-of-the-box layouts and navigation like JavaScript scrolling and other kinds of original layouts. Most portfolios have traditional block-style layouts, with two to three clearly separated columns and a simple, convenient navigation menu.

Number of columns

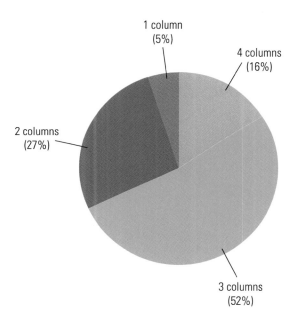

1 column
(5%)

4 columns
(16%)

2 columns
(27%)

3 columns
(52%)

Also, most portfolio websites consist of multiple detailed pages with relatively deep sub-sections. Minimalist one-page portfolios were rare: only 5.4% of the portfolio websites we saw have simple and minimalist designs.

INTRODUCTORY BLOCK ON TOP?

Portfolio websites commonly have a large introductory block in the header of the page, essentially a short friendly statement about what the agency offers and what advantages a customer will gain by using its services. The block usually blends vivid imagery with big typography. It conveys both the company's overall image and the personal tone of the agency's staff, making it equally professional and friendly. Such blocks usually appear immediately below the logo on the front page.

Introductory block at the top?

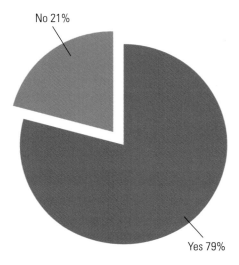

No 21%

Yes 79%

According to our study, 79% of portfolio websites have some kind of introductory block in the upper region. We noticed, though, that some portfolios forgo an introductory block in favor of showcasing recent projects. In such designs, a small "About us" block is placed somewhere else on the page, often below the fold.

LAYOUT ALIGNMENT

Back in '90s, website layouts were traditionally left-aligned, with either vertical navigation in the left sidebar or horizontal navigation near the head. With growing adoption of widescreen displays, this has changed. More and more designers are horizontally centering their layouts so that the passive white space around the page balances the layout.

We did notice a trend towards more original, even right-aligned, layouts at the beginning of the year, but not a single portfolio in our current survey has a right-aligned layout.

Layout alignment

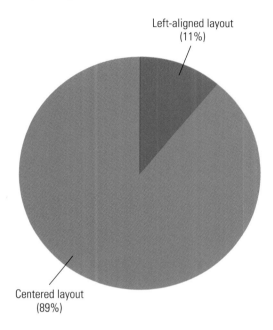

Left-aligned layout
(11%)

Centered layout
(89%)

According to our study,

- No portfolio layouts are right-aligned.
- 89% of portfolio layouts are horizontally centered.
- The rest have either original adaptive layouts, a vivid background image that fills the remaining screen space, or just empty space — of course, you would see the remaining screen space only if your display has a widescreen resolution.

NAVIGATION ALIGNMENT

Where to put the main navigation in the layout? The question isn't trivial and often leads to debate among designers. Surprisingly, our study revealed that most portfolio designers place the main navigation in the upper-right corner of the layout. In fact:

- 80% of portfolios have large horizontal navigation.
- 51% of websites have horizontal navigation with right-aligned elements.

- 16.4% have horizontal navigation with left-aligned elements.
- 11% have full-width horizontal navigation with large clickable elements.

Vertical navigation is rarely used, and other approaches (such as horizontal navigation at the bottom of the page) are found on unconventional out-of-the-box layouts, though still uncommon.

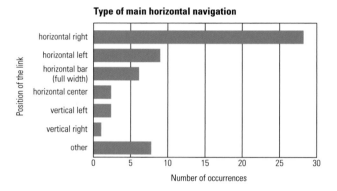

SEARCH BOX DESIGN

While many portfolio websites are quite small, presenting visitors with only some general information about the studio and its design process, some portfolios go the length and present a variety of case studies, blogs, and detailed information about their every major project.

In general, if a website contains a lot of information, search functionality would very likely benefit some visitors to the website. As it turns out, very few companies integrate search functionality into their website.

- 89% of the portfolio websites we studied have no search functionality.
- Only 11% of websites have a search box, usually a simple clean one. Most of the owners of these portfolios have a blog that they update regularly.

FLASH ELEMENTS

Flash, an established tool for rich interactive design, seems to be losing popularity among Web designers — at least among designers of portfolio websites. The reason is probably that certain Flash effects can be replaced by advanced JavaScript techniques, which are often available from popular JavaScript libraries as easy-to-use plug-ins.

Slideshows, animation effects, and transition effects can now be created with JavaScript solutions that are lightweight and quicker and much easier than Flash. Rich Flash animation and video effects are being replaced by simpler, subtler JavaScript techniques. Flash is still sometimes used, though — for instance, for dynamic text replacement.

In our study, only 3.7% of portfolio websites used Flash heavily, and even then usually for slideshows and presentations. The reason is very likely that we did not include any interactive motion design agencies, Flash design studios, or video production studios in our study.

WHERE TO PUT CONTACT INFORMATION?

One important objective of our study was to understand how designers convey information about contact options. Do visitors have to click on a "Contact us" button to get in touch with a design agency? Or is contact information placed prominently at the top of the page? Or do most designers put contact information in the footer — where most users expect it anyway?

The websites we analyzed put contact information in almost every area of the page: top, right, left, bottom, even the middle. But we also noticed some interesting patterns — note that we were interested in, first, where the link to the "Contact us" page was located and, secondly, where the actual contact information itself was positioned.

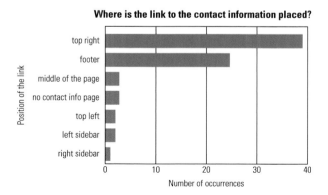

It turns out that:

- Only 12.7% of websites display a phone number in the header of the page.
- Only 9.1% of websites display an email address in the header.

- A postal address usually isn't displayed at all (54.5%) or else is placed in the footer (40%) or upper area of the website (5.4%).
- A "Contact" link usually appears in the upper-right corner (71%) and/or in the footer (45.4%).
- "Contact" (59.7%) and "Contact us" (21%) are the most popular wordings for the link to the Contact page.

Wording for the link to the Contact page

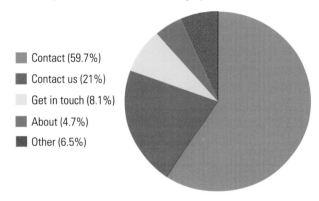

- Contact (59.7%)
- Contact us (21%)
- Get in touch (8.1%)
- About (4.7%)
- Other (6.5%)

"ABOUT US" PAGE

The About page is used on portfolio websites to present the members of the team, explain the philosophy of the agency, and display the company's expertise and professionalism. The page gives the design studio a personal touch and — if designed properly — elicits the trust of potential customers.

An About page is clearly a must for portfolios: 89% of those we analyzed included a link to the page in their main navigation.

The level of detail you use to describe your agency is, of course, up to you. 59.1% of About pages we surveyed have no sub-pages and offer visitors a brief, compact overview. Photos of team members, their personal information and information about the design process are very common on such pages. The tone of the main copy is usually informal, friendly, and sometimes even funny. The most popular wordings for the link to the page is "About" (43.6%), "About us" (27.3%), and "Who we are" (7.2%).

CLIENT PAGE

One of the surest signs of professionalism and a good reputation in the industry is a solid list of clients with whom your company has worked. Of course, the more prominent the companies in the list, the more likely potential customers will give you their attention. In our experience, many customers seek out a client list, case studies, and testimonials when searching for a design agency. So we were surprised to find that only a few agencies have a standalone page listing their clients.

Of the portfolios we analyzed, only 47.2% have a Client page (either as a standalone page or part of a portfolio page). In most cases, clients are represented by their logos, which are often linked to detailed case studies that discuss the work done by the agency and client testimonials. The most popular wording for the link to this page is "Our clients" (46.1%), "Clients" (39.6%), and "Client list" (15.4%).

SERVICES PAGE

Given that visitors usually come to such websites because they are looking for services, validating their search with clear introductory text on the front page or with a standalone Services page is reasonable. Potential clients usually have a pretty good understanding of what they are looking for (motion design, print design, Web design, CD/DVD jacket design, etc.), so putting your major offerings on the Services page is a good idea.

67.2% of the portfolios we looked at have a standalone Services page of some kind. The rest put their information on the About page or the front page. The Services pages sometimes have sub-pages (35.1%), but in most cases the single page is quite long and detailed.

Linking your Portfolio page to your Services page is definitely a good idea because it bridges theory and practice and shows exactly what your agency is capable of. The most popular wording for links to such pages is "Services" or "Our Services" (75.7%), followed by "What we do" (10.8%).

PORTFOLIO PAGE

Potential customers obviously want to see what a design agency is capable of. Does its style match theirs? What aesthetic does it communicate for visual design, typography, and usability? Do its designs feel intuitive and look pleasant? These are the questions potential customers want answered when

19

they become interested in a design agency. So, a solid showcase of previous work could close the deal and convince them to contact the agency.

In general, be selective with the work you showcase, and let visitors order and filter the projects by style, industry, and year. Also provide some information about each project, or even conduct a detailed case study with testimonials and insight into your workflow. Unfortunately, few portfolios do that.

According to our study:

- 7.2% of websites don't have a portfolio at all.
- 12.7% have only logos or screenshots, without any description or case study.
- 16.4% briefly describe each project next to a logo and/or screenshot.
- 63.6% have a very detailed page for each project, including case study, testimonials, slideshow of screenshots, drafts, and sketches.
- Surprisingly, the most popular wording for the link to the Portfolio page is "Work" or "Our work" (47.2%), followed by "Portfolio" (27.2%).

WORKFLOW PAGE

Actually, the Workflow page works rather well as a sub-section of the About page, rather than as a standalone page. However, some designers want to make their explanation of their workflow more prominent. While 74.5% of websites do not have a Workflow page at all, the rest go to rather great lengths to explain to potential customers how their process works and what expectations both parties should have.

Giving potential customers a better understanding of how they will be involved throughout the design process is certainly a good idea. The most popular wordings for the link to this page are "How we work" or "Working with us" (42.8%), "Process" or "Our process" (35.7%), and "Approach" (7.1%).

CONTACT PAGE

If everything goes right, and your portfolio has earned the interest of visitors, then the Contact page will be their final destination. Do everything you can to make it as easy as possible for them to contact you. Make sure customers can provide all necessary information by presenting a simple, clean form that can accommodate the essential information about their project. You could also provide your phone number, postal address, and email address — the more, the better. Driving directions, social profile buttons, and vCards are a good idea, too.

According to our study:

- 9% of websites don't have a Contact page (instead, contact information is included in the footer of each page).
- Driving directions (often with an interactive Google map) are given on 45.4% of portfolio websites.
- 83.6% provide a phone number and email address on the Contact page.
- 76.7% provide a postal address on the contact page.
- 69% of websites have a contact Web form.
- 14.5% offer a vCard for downloading, usually next to the email address.
- Links to social networking websites such as Facebook, Twitter, and LinkedIn are often used (14.5%).

SPECIALS AND EXTRAS

We also noticed a few distinctive elements that some design agencies offer potential customers. One popular approach is to offer some kind of project or proposal request form, which prospective clients are expected to fill out with key details when submitting a request. Also, some design agencies offer a project planner or help customers estimate costs or offer a more detailed pricing guide.

Among the other interesting things we noticed were chat windows on the Contact page (e.g. Agami Creative), a "Stress-o-meter" that displays the company's current availability, a quote calculator, and a "Capabilities and Credentials" presentation (usually in PDF).

OTHER FINDINGS

We also found that:

- None of the portfolio websites have an FAQ page.
- 76.3% of websites have at least one blog, and many portfolios have two or more blogs.
- 14.55% have a newsletter or mailing list.
- 9% provide a detailed site map.

SUMMARY

To summarize our key findings:

- 82% of the portfolio websites we analyzed have a light design, with neutral, calm colors.
- 79% have traditional "block" layouts, with two to three columns clearly separated and a simple, conveniently located navigation menu.
- 79% of websites have some kind of introductory block in the upper area.
- 89% have horizontally centered layouts.
- 80% have large horizontal navigation.
- 51% have horizontal navigation with right-aligned elements.
- 89% do not have search functionality.
- Only 3.7% use Flash heavily throughout the website.
- A contact link appears in the upper-right corner 71% of the time, and/or in the footer 45.4% of the time.
- 89% link to the About page in the main navigation.
- Only 47.2% have a Client page.
- 67.2% of portfolios have some form of standalone Services page.
- 63.6% have a detailed page for each project, including case study, testimonials, slideshow with screenshots, drafts, and sketches.
- 74.5% of websites have no Workflow page.
- The Contact page should contain driving directions, a phone number, email address, postal address, vCard, and online form.

Vitaly Friedman is Editor-In-Chief of Smashing Magazine.

3

CREATING A SUCCESSFUL ONLINE PORTFOLIO

By Sean Hodge

YOUR PORTFOLIO IS the showcase of your work, skills and potential for future employers. The more time and effort you dedicate to creating a usable and good-looking design, the higher your chances of getting a better account balance at the end of the month. So how do you make sure your portfolio is better than that of competitors? How do you draw the attention of employers to your work?

Creating a successful portfolio is easier than you think. Make it simple and easy to use and hit your objectives, and you'll end up with a successful portfolio. In this article, we'll review five pitfalls that plague portfolio designs. Then we'll cover portfolio tips that, if carefully heeded and executed well, will deliver quality results.

Let's review the common mistakes that designers make to ensure that you don't fall into one of these traps.

PITFALL #1: OBFUSCATING

Clarity and focus should permeate your portfolio. Don't use twenty words when seven would do. Push your best content to the front. Where possible, place important content above the fold. Avoid meandering in your language. Don't make the levels of your portfolio too deep, but make sure that the section still accomplishes your objectives.

Copyblogger.com has an article that features a simple list of writing tips based on the early 20th-century writer known for cutting out the fluff. See the article "Ernest Hemingway's Top 5 Tips for Writing Well" (`www.copyblogger.com/ernest-hemingway-top-5-tips-for-writing-well`). Hemingway championed short sentences, strong forceful language, and clarity: all principles that make for effective writing on the Web.

In the article "Creating The Perfect Portfolio" (`www.digital-web.com/articles/the_perfect_portfolio`), Collis Ta'eed offers portfolio advice from the perspective of a potential employer. The section titled "Get to it" gives reasons for limiting the number of portfolio pieces you present and for making your best pieces easy to find. An employer has to review many applicants quickly. You are more likely to make the cut if your best work is prominent. The portfolio of Evan Eckard (`www.evaneckard.com/`) is an example of a website that promotes his best work right on the first page and "gets to it" quickly.

PITFALL #2: CRAMMING INFORMATION

Another pitfall is wanting to say too much in too little space. You need to achieve a balance in the number of pages users have to click for more information and the amount of information you fit on a page. Be aware of this when constructing your portfolio.

The more tightly packed your portfolio, the more likely it will look cluttered. If you do need to put a lot of information on the page, consult the post "Grid and Column Designs" on WebDesigner Wall (`www.webdesignerwall.com/trends/grid-and-column-designs`). It will give you some great ideas on how to use the grid to your advantage when presenting a lot of information.

PITFALL #3: OVERDOING IT

You're less likely to go wrong by keeping things simple and organized. Do this for all areas of your portfolio. Less is more. The more you try to do in your portfolio, the more likely things will go wrong.

Showcasing 18 of your services will be less successful than prioritizing a few. Too many types of work or too much work of a single type will likely drown users. They won't spot those prominent pieces that show how great your work is.

PITFALL #4: UNUSUAL NAVIGATION

Designers have an urge to stand out as unique. The last place to act on this urge is in your website's navigation. It's a numbers game. If enough visitors to your portfolio have difficulty navigating it, the portfolio will have failed to achieve its goals.

In the post "My Last Portfolio Sucked, Yours Might Too," (`http://astheria.com/design/my-last-portfolio-sucked-yours-might-too`), Kyle Meyer points out some perfect examples of navigation choices to avoid. He reviews 200 portfolios, and points out their problems. Navigation accounted for over 32% of the problems.

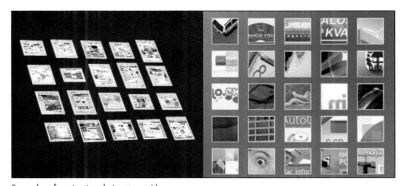

Examples of navigation choices to avoid

PITFALL #5: VISUAL CLUTTER

Consider the purpose of any decorative element. If it meets your goals and complements your work, then great. Otherwise, remove it. White space lends a professional feel to your portfolio. The more elements you cram into an area, the more difficult it will be to maintain a semblance of professionalism.

Use hierarchy to guide users through the page. On boxesandarrows.com, the article "Visible Narratives: Understanding Visual Organization" by Luke Wroblewski explains the principles related to visual hierarchy (`www.boxesandarrows.com/view/visible_narratives_understanding_visual_organization`).

And in the interview "Where Visual Design Meets Usability" (`www.uie.com/articles/wroblewski_interview`), both page hierarchy and visual clutter are addressed. In this interview, Wroblewski references some of Edward Tufte's teachings on avoiding superfluous data.

PRINCIPLES OF EFFECTIVE PORTFOLIO DESIGN

In the following pages you'll find some suggestions for improving your portfolio (or getting it right the first time from scratch). Bear in mind that some of these suggestions require patience, time, and a lot of planning. But they're worth it. And the examples provided show that one can achieve outstanding results just by following these 12 simple rules.

DEFINE YOUR CRITERIA AND STRATEGIES FOR SUCCESS

As with any project, clarify your goals before beginning. Once you know your goals, then every decision you make will be affected. Following are some common portfolio goals. Also, be aware that portfolios are often meant to accomplish more than one goal. You may need to consider creating multiple portfolios for different purposes.

- The *hire me portfolio* focuses on getting you a job. If you are actively searching for employment, then the primary goal of your portfolio is to get you hired. You can target this type of portfolio to the type of company you want to work for.
- The *sales generation portfolio* focuses on keeping the flow of work coming through the door. The goal here is to generate leads and move potential customers through the sales channel.

- The *reputation-building portfolio* builds your name in the industry and online. This could take the form of an artist's showcase, or you could tie your work together in a portfolio blog.

- The *networking portfolio* builds relationships. Many networks have excellent portfolio-building tools and offer some advantages to placing your portfolio on their website. Chief among them is leveraging the website's space for networking.

CONSIDER MULTIPLE PORTFOLIOS

There are multiple reasons to have more than one portfolio. You may have more than one skill set to promote. You may want to send one portfolio to a particular marketing director to land you a specific job. The director will appreciate that. It saves them time and shows that you really want the job — even if it's a one-page portfolio.

Even if you fill the second portfolio with the same work, you will still benefit by targeting your portfolios to different groups.

Take the case of Nik Ainley, a UK-based designer and illustrator. He has multiple portfolios that all serve complementary goals. He participates in multiple portfolio-based communities to build his reputation and to network with other designers. His website, Shiny Binary, has received over 1 million visits.

Nik has a portfolio on Behance (www.behance.net/shinybinary). He's involved in numerous groups there and has a large inner circle. The portfolio prominently communicates that he is available for freelancing, long-term contracts, full-time work, and consulting jobs.

He also has a very popular portfolio on DeviantArt (http://shinybinary .deviantart.com/). He's been a member there since 2004 and now has over 80 portfolio pieces and over 1,000 comments on his work. A lot of fans have marked his works as favorites.

Though less active on Gallery on CPLUV, he does a portfolio there, too (www.cpluv.com/profile/users/shinybinary). And his portfolio on Depthcore (http://depthcore.com/artist/Nik+Ainley/) is good. That website features only artists whose works have been solicited, so the quality is high.

Shiny Binary, the website of Nik Ainley

Overall, Nik Ainley shows how one can benefit from having multiple portfolios online, even when the work being showcased in the portfolios is similar. He is tapping into a different community with each one. By doing this yourself, you're making connections with new people and exposing them to your work.

TARGET YOUR MARKET

The more targeted your design is to a specific market, the more it will speak to the people in that market. If you are looking to land corporate clients in a conservative industry, then present them with clean, marketable, and professional work. Don't showcase edgy, grungy, or arty work unless that's the market you're going after.

The article "The Secret to Getting a Lot of Web Design Work" by Colin Ta'eed (`http://freelanceswitch.com/designer/the-secret-to-getting-a-lot-of-web-design-work/`) has a section entitled "Design the portfolio you think your clients want to see." And that is precisely the point. Focus your portfolio on your target market. If you're trying to get certain clients, then design with those clients in mind.

There are yet more benefits to targeting a market. In the article "Finding a Target Market" (`http://www.digitaloutput.net/content/ContentCT.asp?P=843`), Barbara Pellow discusses both vertical and horizontal approaches to target marketing. She identifies some of the other benefits of target marketing. Speaking to a specific audience allows you to become a recognized expert in the field more easily. Targeting a market differentiates your services.

Consider the example of a Web designer who specializes in creating law firm website. His target market will be different than that of a designer who builds rock band websites. The language, graphics, and approach of their respective portfolios will differ greatly. A Web designer who has numerous successful law firm websites in his portfolio will make it easier for other potential law firm clients to choose him over another designer or agency.

Designers are more likely to stand out by targeting a specific market. Their success rate at landing niche jobs and being perceived as experts in their field will increase. Take Dan Gilroy's portfolio (`www.dangilroy.com/portfolio.htm`) as an example of one that successfully targets a particular market.

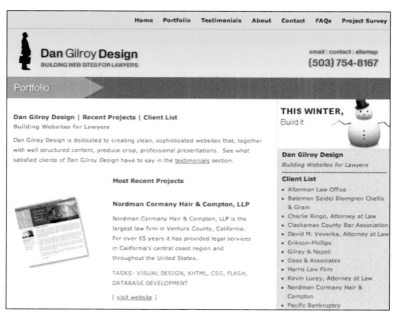

Target the look of your portfolio to your intended market.

Copyright © 2010 Dan Gilroy Design, LLC

Having a target market is essential to selecting portfolio pieces and designing your website.

PRIORITIZE USABILITY

Navigation is of paramount importance. See the earlier point about unusual navigation. Another consideration is Web standards. This is especially relevant if you're currently looking for a job. Read the article "Five Steps to a Better Design Portfolio" by Jeffrey Veen (`www.veen.com/jeff/archives/000935.html`). In it, Veen discusses best practices for portfolios in the context of how you will be perceived by employers.

Also, don't discount search bots. Work toward better search engine optimization. The blog SEOBook (`www.seobook.com/blog`) is a rich resource on the topic. Good SEO improves the ability of potential clients to find you in search engines.

USE THE RIGHT TECHNOLOGY

If certain technologies are fixtures of the job descriptions you're interested in, then it makes sense to build your portfolio with that technology. Sure Flash is cool, but is it right for your website? Probably not if you're a logo designer. But if you're trying to land a job as a Flash designer at a top-notch interactive design agency, then it's the right choice.

The navigation in the portfolio of new media designer Matthew V. Robinson (`www.matthewvrobinson.com/`) is easy to use. Speed is essential to the success of a Flash website. Matthew's portfolio is highly usable and looks great.

Consider maintainability when deciding on technologies. Simplifying your portfolio as much as possible will reduce the time you spend upgrading and making changes.

How easy is it to add and remove portfolio pieces? The easier it is, the more likely you'll update the portfolio regularly. Jamie Gregory (`www.jamiegregory.co.uk`) has a simple, elegant, and effective one-page portfolio. He would have no trouble adding or swapping out pieces.

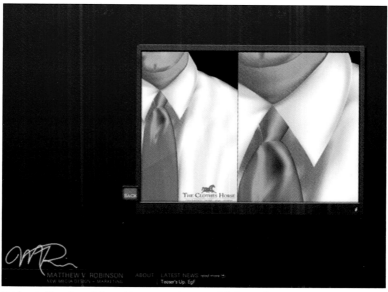

Matthew Robinson's portfolio combines easy navigation and flashy graphics.

Consider enhancement when looking at technology. A wise choice is often to add just a little JavaScript or other technology, rather than rely on them heavily. It will help achieve your goals without complicating your design. On Marius Roosendaal's portfolio (www.mariusroosendaal.com/), take a moment to explore how clean the source code is, complemented by the elegant JavaScript-based solutions.

Think before choosing between a static website and a content management system. One-page portfolios are easy to update and a quick way to show your best work. You'll also have no issues with navigation, with only one page. But you'll have little flexibility, and you won't be able to leverage the additional features that content management systems have to promote your work, like a blog.

PLAN THE PROJECT

A key factor in creating a successful portfolio is to approach it as you would a client project. Manage the project as professionally as you would any other Web project you take on. Set aside sufficient time to achieve the goals you've outlined. Make sure also to set deadlines to keep you on track.

LIMIT THE SCOPE AND TYPE OF WORK YOU PROMOTE

Your portfolio should be limited to your best work within the scope of your goals. If you are looking to do website redesigns, then your portfolio should consist only of those, not logo designs or print work you may have done. If you're not looking for a particular type of work, then don't showcase it. You will be more successful.

Jesse Bennett-Chamberlain redesigned his website, 31three.com, back in May 2007. He used to have print and logo designs in his portfolio. In the redesign, he clarified his target market by focusing on providing design assistance to developers.

His current portfolio presents only website and interface designs because that is the type of work he is looking for. This portfolio is very successful on many fronts and has been cited throughout the blogosphere.

That doesn't mean that Jesse doesn't do logo or identity design. He does, but he recognizes that logo design is not why people come to him. They come to him for designs for new or existing websites; logo design might happen to be part of the package. See more about his process in the article "Redesigning the ExpressionEngine Site" (www.digital-web.com/articles/redesigning_the_expressionengine_site/).

Certainly some designers and firms will have mixed bags. The more types of work you do well, the greater the challenge you'll have in promoting that work. When possible, keep the work on display to a minimum. Ten of your best pieces often work better than fifty good pieces.

PROVIDE ADEQUATE CONTACT INFORMATION, DOCUMENTATION, AND EXPLANATIONS

Contact information should be easy to find, and contact forms should be easy to use. Make this information prominent. The Hicksdesign portfolio (www.hicksdesign.co.uk/) displays contact information clearly on every page.

Each page of the Hicksdesign website displays a contact link.
© Hicksdesign Ltd 2002-10

Clarifying your role in the projects in your portfolio instills confidence in potential clients. If you designed a website but someone else coded it, state that. If you did everything, then confidently declare that, too. Cameron Moll (www.cameronmoll.com/portfolio/) demonstrates this principle.

Case studies give a deeper view into your process. Once a potential client has narrowed their list, they may come back to spend more time on your portfolio. Case studies show how competent and thorough your process is. David Airey makes his case studies easy to find (www.davidairey.com/miskeeto-logo-design/).

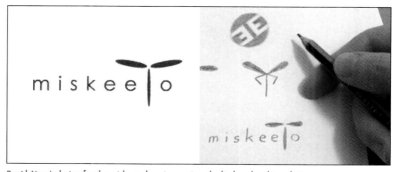

David Airey's design for the miskeeto logo is prominently displayed on his website.

Client testimonials are effective in persuading visitors that you deliver on promises. They increase professionalism when tastefully incorporated in a portfolio. David Airey's article "The Importance of Client Testimonials" (`www.davidairey.com/the-importance-of-client-testimonials/`) has useful information on the subject.

PRESENT YOUR WORK IN THE CONTEXT OF YOUR GOALS

Your work should stand out the most in your portfolio. If the design or page layout overpowers the work on display, then you're not likely to meet your goals. Consider every visual element that you add to the page carefully. When unsure, favor simplicity.

INFUSE YOUR PERSONALITY IN THE DESIGN

Nick La's portfolio captures his design style and interests. The unique background illustration stands out. It doesn't impede usability but acts as a beautiful wrapper. For some, this would interfere too much with the work being presented (though it works fine in his portfolio).

In his famous 2009 design, Nick sets his pieces against a solid white background in a strong column-based design. The work shown suits the background illustration. Pulling off this kind of infusion of personality is difficult, but it makes your portfolio not only memorable but remarkable.

Nick has achieved tremendous success with his N.Design Studio portfolio (`www.ndesign-studio.com/portfolio`). Infusing personality in a design ultimately means giving expression to the aesthetic you have been cultivating over the years.

Seth Godin makes some excellent points about being remarkable in his post "How to Be Remarkable" (`http://sethgodin.typepad.com/seths_blog/2007/01/how_to_be_remar.html`). He says, "Remarkability lies in the edges: the biggest, fastest, slowest, richest, easiest, most difficult." This is a good point, but in pursuing that edge, you run the huge risk of riding right off the cliff.

Nick La's personality permeates his portfolio.

© N.Design Studio 2010

Carefully consider how you will blend such remarkable personal elements into your portfolio without sacrificing usability and without upsetting the balance between the prominence of your portfolio and the overall website design.

PROMOTE AND LEVERAGE YOUR WORK

There are many ways to promote your portfolio. Consider joining professional online communities to network with other members. We've already mentioned some communities where you can submit a portfolio. Add a thread to a design forum about your portfolio. Submit your design to gallery websites. Almost any strategy for promoting a website can be used to promote a portfolio.

Add a blog to your website. The more traffic you draw to your website, the more exposure your portfolio will get. Dan Cederholm was an early adopter of this strategy and achieved fame with his blog Simplebits (`http://simplebits.com/`). His portfolio resides successfully on the same website.

Leveraging your work involves linking to it when you send emails. Add a link to your portfolio in your Facebook profile or any other community you belong to. Integrate your portfolio into your communications and online identity.

DEVELOP LONG-TERM GOALS

Having a vision of the future always helps. Your needs will evolve as you take on different projects over the course of your career. All the same, looking at the recent past can also affect the choices you make in creating your portfolio.

A successful portfolio finds that perfect blend of personality, prominence, simplicity, and ease of use. Make your portfolio stand out from the crowd and serve your goals.

Sean Hodge is the creative mind behind AiBURN, a weblog about design, creativity, inspiration, and graphics.

BETTER USER EXPERIENCE WITH STORYTELLING

By Francisco Inchauste

STORIES DEFINE OUR world. They have been with us since the dawn of communication, from cave walls to the tall tales recounted around fires. They continue to evolve, but their purpose remains the same: to entertain, share common experiences, teach, and pass on traditions.

Today we communicate a bit differently. Our information is fragmented across various mass-media channels and delivered through ever-changing technology. It has become watered down, cloned, and is churned out quickly in 140-character blurbs. We've lost that personal touch where we find an emotional connection that makes us care.

Using storytelling, however, we can pull these fragments together in a common thread. We can connect as real people, not just computers. In this chapter, we explore how user experience professionals and designers are *using storytelling to create compelling experiences* that build human connections.

IT BEGINS WITH A STORY

In 1977, a simple story turned the film industry on its head. The special effects technology used to construct this story had not been created or used in filmmaking prior to its release. The author disregarded what was popular and marketable at the time (apocalyptic and disaster movies) to follow his own vision. The film starred unknown actors, and the genre was a relic of 1930s serial movies. It was turned down by many film studios and at one point almost shelved.

The movie, if you haven't yet guessed, is *Star Wars*. The author is George Lucas. *Star Wars* went on to become one of the most successful films of all time and a pop culture phenomenon. It inaugurated the blockbuster trilogy and completely changed the way special effects were done. Many of today's most influential film companies were spawned from the success of these movies: LucasFilm, THX, Industrial Light & Magic (ILM), and Pixar.

Star Wars wasn't a new story, though. It drew on the mythic archetypes from stories told over thousands of years.

REVEALING THE DESIGN IN STORIES

The creation of a story is often viewed as an almost magical or random process. The author sits in front of his canvas, the blank word processor, and begins to type whatever inspires him at the moment. Great stories, though, don't just happen randomly; they are designed. There is a pattern at work here. In order to be entertaining, find the right dramatic cues, and tap deep into our collective psyche, a writer must follow a specific method. The arc of a typical story is illustrated in the following figure. A story that fails to pull in the audience emotionally and hold their attention probably did not use enough of these patterns as a guide.

This story structure has been around since long before screenwriting was taught. There was a point when it remained simply an unnoticed rhythm in the background of every story. Some aspects of this structure — such as the hero's journey and comparative mythology — were first popularized by Joseph Campbell. He wrote about his studies in the book *The Hero with a Thousand Faces*.

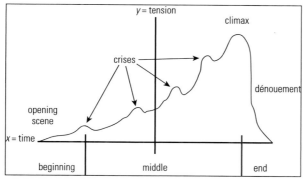

The story "arc" is widely used in screenwriting and novels.

Campbell was a disciple of Swiss psychiatrist Carl Jung, who believed that we are all born with a subconscious idea of what a "hero," "mentor," and "quest" should be. He studied the structure of religions and myths across many cultures. He discovered that, consciously or not, every story (or myth) was created with the same basic formula. This is why great stories transcend even language barriers. This assessment by Campbell set off large ripples in the waters of myth and religion.

The stories that captivate us on the silver screen and in novels follow these same patterns. We talk about dialogue and scenes at the water cooler as if they happened to a personal friend, rather than a fictional character, all because we become emotionally invested in the characters and story.

Brands strive for this emotional investment every day. Starbucks doesn't just want to sell us coffee — it wants customers to become invested in its story: the ambience, aromas, community. Its goal is to become the "third abode" (home, work, Starbucks). It claims that, "It's really about the human connection."

THE POWER OF EMOTION

When speaking of stories, we typically describe an emotional experience, something that affects us at a very personal level. This is much different than the way we usually describe our experience with products such as websites and applications. These are seen more as utilitarian and task-oriented.

If we are able to accomplish what we set out to do— say, transfer money in a banking application — then it has been a good user experience. In order to achieve our goals, the interface should be usable and should function the way we expect. This view is preached by many usability experts, including Donald Norman, professor of cognitive science and a usability consultant for the Nielsen Norman Group.

Upon hearing people say that if his rules were followed, then "everything would be ugly," Norman decided to explore people's relationship to design. The result was the book *Emotional Design*.

Through his research, Norman found that design affects how people experience products, which happens at three different levels and translates into three types of design:

- *Visceral design:* This design is from a subconscious and biologically pre-wired level of thinking. We might automatically dislike certain things (spiders, rotten smells, etc.) and like others ("attractive" people, symmetrical objects, etc.). This is our initial reaction to appearance.
- *Behavioral design:* This is how the product or application functions, the look and feel, the usability — our total experience with using it.
- *Reflective design:* This is how the product or application makes us feel after the initial impact and interaction, where we associate it with our broader life experience and attach meaning and value to it.

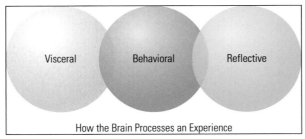

Visceral   Behavioral   Reflective

How the Brain Processes an Experience

We process design at three different levels.

There is a lot more to emotion than can be covered here, but understanding these basic levels of processing gives us some insight into why storytelling is so powerful. Consider how the levels play off each other at an amusement park: people pay to be scared. At the visceral level, we have a fear of heights and danger. At the behavioral level, we trust that it is safe to go on the ride;

and at the reflective level, we anticipate that emotionally charged rush and sense of accomplishment (in overcoming our fear of heights) when the ride is over.

Given how vital emotion is to how we think, it becomes all the more important not just to create a functional and usable experience but to seek out and create a meaningful connection.

THE BASICS OF STORYTELLING FOR USER EXPERIENCE

At a basic level, storytelling and user experience have common elements — planning, research, and content creation — that can be used to create a satisfying experience. Storytelling offers a way for a team to really understand the product it is building and the audience it is building it for.

Stories enable the most complex of ideas to be effectively communicated to people. This crafted product or experience then delivers meaning and emotion to its users. Professionals who currently exploit the power of narrative in their projects do so in vastly different ways. The following sections outline some of the modern uses and benefits of storytelling.

BRINGING TEAMS TOGETHER

User experience professionals typically have to work with people from many different backgrounds. Depending on the type of experience needed, a project may require a range of skills, from an engineer to a user interface designer. And the approach often taken in creating websites or applications is to first consider the technology, or the limits of that technology. To make matters more complex, members of large teams tend be preoccupied with their respective domains; for example, the marketing person will focus on his own objectives and strategies based on his experience. This is not always in the end user's best interest and often results in a poor, diluted experience.

The user experience team selected to create an iPhone application for the masses would be quite different than the one selected to develop a medical device for doctors. As mentioned, the experts at crafting stories know how to tap into a way of communicating that has been around for thousands of years. Using storytelling, user experience teams can also inject emotion and value into their product for users.

PURSUING A USER-CENTERED GOAL

In hearing about the storytelling approach, one might think that it's just another way of talking about "strategy." But storytelling carries with it a more user-centered goal. Companies like Apple have used similar methods in their design process to really define what they are building.

Cindy Chastain refers to it as an experience theme. She says this theme is "the core value of the experience" being offered. Christian Saylor refers to it as finding the lead character. Without this user-centered goal, he states, we are just "designing for the sake of designing."

Oriented around a specific theme or character, the otherwise uncoordinated elements of an experience all merge into a clear goal and purpose. With storytelling, a diverse team creating a website or application can collectively link the tangible elements and create something that is a meaningful experience, more than just bits and bytes.

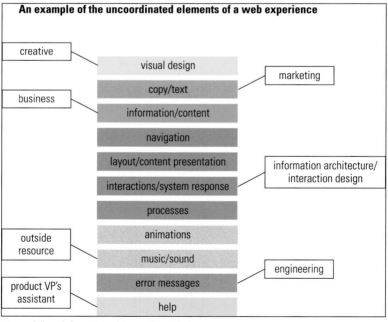

Diverse skills and elements combine to tell a unified story.

DEFINING THE USER

A lot of discussion and articles are circulating about usability and functionality on websites and in applications. Functionality, of course, is important.
For instance, what good is an airplane if the engine isn't powerful enough to
get it off the ground? If you step back though, the more important question
is, how far does the passenger need to go? If it's only a few miles down the
road, then it really doesn't matter if the plane is functional: it's the wrong
solution altogether. So, identifying what we really need to build is key in the
initial phase of building the user experience.

When the research is finished, we typically move on to create personas as
a way to understanding the user; this process can be regarded as part of
creating the story. By building an imagined representation of the user based
on real research and observation, we are able to empathize with users and
truly understand their needs. By creating stories around these personas, we
are able to conceive a more meaningful vision of the project.

Storytelling allows us to translate this research into anecdotes, making it
easier for people to grasp and recall meaning. In addition, being able to
empathize with users through stories helps us better understand the
emotional side of the experience. Films and video games deliver experiences
that affect people at an emotional level. Users are beginning to expect similar
experiences from the websites and applications they use every day.

We can thus shift our focus from creating simple task-driven websites and
applications to cultivating valuable human connections. This is, after all, a
"global campfire" as Curt Cloninger refers to it (`www.alistapart.com/`
`articles/storytelling/`). He goes on to say, "The Web is not a global
network of connected computers. The Web is a global network of connected
people. And storytelling is still the most effective way to emotionally impact
people."

THE BENEFITS

Most projects have a lot of documentation outlining their goals and
strategies. These come in the form of business requirements, functional
documentation, and other supporting research and information. Storytelling
can improve the overall product/experience by doing the following:

- Putting a human face to dry data
- Simplifying complex ideas for the team

43

- Making team collaboration more efficient
- Clarifying purpose
- Gaining insight into primary users
- Setting a project's direction more quickly
- Facilitating communication within large organizations
- Delivering meaning and value to users

Storytelling helps teams focus on everything from website content to understanding their business problem in a new way. For example, you could quickly define a project's scope without designing or wireframing screens. The UX team for Yahoo! Personals created a story about a fictional dating couple going through certain scenarios. Through this story, the team was able to better understand the purpose of the website and the type of experience users should go through. It opened up the task- and strategy-based steps to the more authentic and emotional experience of dating. It was a powerful way to get the team to speak directly "to" the experience, rather than create documentation "around" it.

HAPPILY EVER AFTER: THE REALITY

There are many different opinions on how best to craft the user experience. Many of them stem from the basic approaches developed by Alan Cooper, a pioneer in building software with user-driven experiences (www.cooper.com). But as technology evolves, so do the approaches and processes used to create solutions that meet users' needs. The number of approaches to user experience is close to the number of frameworks available to develop software. It usually comes down to what is best for the type of projects that a team typically works on.

Your ability to follow a particular process depends on many things, including timeline, budget, and goals. In reality, doing everything as outlined by a specific process is not always possible.

Storytelling is a way to connect teams quickly, to gain insight and understanding. The experiences we create take shape through design, content, and user interaction. Storytellers have been communicating successfully for much longer than websites have been around — which makes storytelling a valuable tool for the business side of design.

A FEW MODERN-DAY STORYTELLERS

Although the idea of using storytelling within the user experience process is fairly new, a few professionals are using it in their projects. I spoke with some of these modern-day storytellers to get their perspectives and see how they are applying storytelling to their work.

DORELLE RABINOWITZ

Dorelle is a storyteller who designs, illustrates, and tells stories in a variety of media and contexts.

Dorelle Rabinowitz (http://www.slideshare.net/dorelvis/storytelling-a-compelling-design-tool)

Question: How do you approach storytelling in UX?

Dorelle: I see it as another tool we can use as a catalyst to communicate during our design activities. For me as a designer, it's about putting a human face to the design process and bringing people together. You can get designers, engineers, product managers, strategists, and execs jazzed about a proposed feature because of a story, and it can be extremely fulfilling. As a person, it's all about the emotional connection.

45

Back in the day, I worked on an Oxygen media website called "Our Stories," where we created short online digital stories with our audience. We called it co-creation, and when I moved more into designing user experiences, I realized that stories helped me understand my users better. As I did more and more work, I realized that storytelling facilitates communication, that people respond emotionally to stories, bond over stories, and share stories again and again, and that the more I integrated storytelling into my work, the better the work was.

So much of what we do isn't only about the design but about how we deal with people, negotiate, and plan. Storytelling can be effective in all of these situations as well as in driving toward solutions. I think the value of stories is independent of the type of experience in which they are used.

Question: In the end, business goals (i.e., profit) rule the day. How does storytelling tie into this?

Dorelle: Stories help bridge understanding, so storytelling can help teams get on the same page and speak the same language — leading to expected results. Stories can help people work more collaboratively and thus help teams get projects done faster, with a faster time to market. Stories can help reframe business problems so that projects solve the right problems and come to better solutions.

Question: Where is the best place to learn more?

Dorelle: Cindy Chastain's article in Boxes and Arrows on "Experience Themes" is a great read (`www.boxesandarrows.com/view/experience-themes`).

CURT CLONINGER

Curt is an artist and writer. He says his art doesn't really tell a standard narrative with a climax and resolution but rather tries to create a kind of event experience.

Question: How do you approach storytelling in UX?

Curt: Design, particularly graphic design, can be understood as a visual form of communication, and storytelling is an historically tested form of communication. Storytelling or narrative design is more like something to keep in mind when considering the user's experience.

To me, narrative design just means having a consistent "voice" and having every design element contribute to the same goal or conclusion. It also means allowing for an arc in the user experience. And it means allowing the user to have some kind of personal say in completing her experience.

This is the difference between a novel (where the user mentally fills in lots of visual blanks) and a Hollywood action film (where all the blanks are filled in for the user). A novel is arguably more engaging.

Curt Cloninger (http://www.lab404.com/dreams/library.html#text)

Question: In the end, business goals (i.e., profit) rule the day. How does storytelling tie into this?

Curt: Hollywood tells stories, and it seems to make a lot of money from it. Politicians, journalists, and large corporations often tell stories (i.e. lies), and they make money. The evolution of any brand over time is a kind of narrative.

Corporations spend all kinds of money trying to convince us that their characters (e.g., Ronald McDonald) are the good guys. Narrative and capitalism have always enjoyed a fruitful relationship.

Question: Where is the best place to learn more?

Curt: I like Nathan Shedroff's *Experience Design* book. It's more about "XD" than "UX," but it addresses narrative at several points throughout. Richard Schechner's *Performance Theory* is good. It has nothing to do with user experience design per se, but it is about theater, tribal ritual, and the cultural interfaces that people construct to give meaning to their worlds.

CHRISTIAN SAYLOR

Christian is a storyteller who designs user experiences. He believes that the things around us have very powerful stories to tell.

Christian Saylor (http://www.undertheinfluenceofdesign.com/2009/06/19/the-art-of-storytelling/)

Question: How do you approach storytelling in UX?

Christian: Storytelling gives us purpose and a sense of place. So, it hasn't been so much a "discovery" of storytelling as a natural progression towards uncovering an experience buried deep within a narrative that wants to be told.

This idea of adopting "storytelling" as a means to uncover a rich experience for the "end" user, whoever they may be, just makes sense.

At the end of the day, the job of the (UX) designer is to help tell a story that is relevant and meaningful, regardless of time, device, or even location. We use "personas" (characters in our story) and "scenarios" (narratives that tell a story about the persona) in order to fully understand not only the target audience but also their goals and desires, which ultimately helps to create a meaningful experience for them.

I strongly believe that everything has a story associated with it. Every business, social group, concept, methodology, and relationship is desperately seeking out better ways to engage with its audience.

Some just happen to do it on a large scale (Apple), while others quietly establish a pattern of life that goes unnoticed until it disappears (the remote control). From packaging that sits on the store shelf to the applications that follow us throughout our days, story influences just about every aspect of our lives. Story is all around us. It gives us a sense of understanding and knowledge of the people and things that are important to us.

I think the most important aspect of storytelling for me is that it has the ability to change the way we view and interact with our world.

Question: In the end, business goals (i.e., profit) rule the day. How does storytelling tie into this?

Christian: If you're telling the right story to the wrong audience, or even telling the right story the wrong way, then your business or product will ultimately fade away. Design and technology are the catalysts of change in the "experience economy." And if we don't seek out better ways to tell our story, then the vitality of our business, product, or service will be jeopardized.

As we all know, the business world is constantly looking at the bottom line. We live in a world saturated by products and services that vie for our attention, and the experience — the way in which a story unfolds — will be the difference between a company's success and failure.

Question: Where is the best place to learn more?

Christian: "Lovemarks (the future beyond brands)" by Saatchi & Saatchi (www.lovemarks.com). It has unbelievable insight into the way we fall in love with the companies and products that surround us.

49

CINDY CHASTAIN

Cindy is a trained filmmaker and screenwriter who makes films and writes scripts and considers herself a visual and dramatic storyteller.

Question: How do you approach storytelling in UX?

Cindy: Storytelling is another discipline that can be used in the context of design as 1) a device, 2) a framework, and/or 3) a craft to draw upon. In other words, we can use story as a way to capture and sell an idea; we can use it as a way to frame an approach to the design of a product or service; or we can use narrative techniques to craft an interaction and, hence, a variety of behavioral and emotional responses to a story.

We tell stories that seek to order chaos, provide meaning, and engage the emotions of our listeners. We design experiences that hopefully do something similar. But in the context of design, meaning is also about what this experience, product, or service will do for a person. It's about how something fits into or enhances his life. It's about understanding how something is supposed to function.

As designers, we do well at facilitating the dialogue between people and the interactive products they use. But we often neglect to consider the more intangible layer of experience, the stories that evolve dynamically through interactions that people have with the things we make.

We also lack an approach to holistic design. If we can learn to approach design more like writers approach stories, we will not only build richer experiences but start to develop a craft in our work that knows how and when certain narrative techniques can be used to engage the minds, emotions, and imaginations of users. Knowing the craft of narrative helps us build better stories, which helps us turn a set of lifeless features and functions into a whole experience that engages the minds and emotions of customers.

Question: In the end, business goals (i.e., profit) rule the day. How does storytelling tie into this?

Cindy: Brand message is no longer the thing that sells. Experience sells. If the intangible pleasure, emotion, or meaning we seek can be made tangible through the use of story and narrative techniques, we will build more compelling product experiences. And if the experience is more compelling, businesses will profit from droves of loyal, experience-discerning customers.

Without this understanding, choices about what features should be included and how they should behave seem both uninspired and disconnected. Sure, we have business goals, user needs, design principles, and best practices to draw on, but these things won't get a team to a place where it is collaborating in the same conceptual space, let alone designing for emotion and meaning.

Question: Where is the best place to learn more?

Cindy: Start with the discipline itself, like *Story,* Robert McKee's book about screenwriting. For a dive into theory, I recommend *Narration in the Fiction Film,* by David Bordwell, and the classic *Computers as Theatre* by Brenda Laurel. And for the first word on storytelling, read *The Poetics* by Aristotle.

THE STORYTELLING EXPERIENCES AROUND US

There are many experiences in which storytelling is used to create a compelling message that draws users in. The stories are not always visible or apparent right away, but underneath many good experiences we find great stories. They can appear in a series of interactions that tie into a larger story or simply in an emotional connection that we form with a product or brand.

51

IN PACKAGING: APPLE

One company that excels at delivering a powerful story is Apple. Purchasing an Apple product and opening the many beautiful layers of packaging follow the typical story arc in building anticipation.

As you move through the process, you find compelling photography and clever writing. These build a sort of satisfying tension until you finally arrive at the climax of the experience and uncover the iPhone. A more common anti-climactic approach would be to wrap the iPhone in bubble plastic, reducing the story to a mere "Buy me."

IN MARKETING: SIX SCENTS PERFUME

The Six Scents range of fragrances (`www.six-scents.com`) is created annually by pairing six prominent artists with six celebrated perfumers. The goal is to help raise awareness for a charitable cause. For the second series, each bottle comes with a DVD that contains a video and photography. The video and imagery create a story around each scent to evoke a certain feeling and theme.

Six Scents Perfume

IN ARCHITECTURE: HBO STORE

The HBO Store (in midtown Manhattan) is designed with storytelling built seamlessly into an immersive experience. The architecture and technology allow the space to become a new way to experience the props and merchandise of HBO shows. The goal for the store (designed in part by design and branding studio Imaginary Forces) was to create an intelligent and memorable experience for visitors.

HBO Store
©2010 Home Box Office, Inc.

IN DATA: TAXI 07: ROADS FORWARD

In her comments on storytelling, Dorelle Rabinowitz shows how storytelling can be used to communicate otherwise boring data and turn it into a more accessible experience. One example of this was Taxi 07: Roads Forward (`www.designtrust.org/publications/publication_07roads fwd.html`). It was a report for the New York City Taxi & Limousine Commission on the current state of the taxi cab industry in New York. The information was presented through stories in comic book form and beautiful infographics.

Taxi Road
©2009 The Design Trust for Public Space

THE END IS THE BEGINNING OF THIS STORY

Many aspects of storytelling and user experience could not be covered in this article. This series is meant to give you a starting point to explore and learn more. The end of this story hasn't been written. This is just the beginning of using storytelling in new ways.

Francisco Inchauste is a UX designer who enjoys writing. You'll find more about his adventures in the world of design and user experience on his blog, Finch (`www.getfinch.com/`*).*

5

DESIGNING USER INTERFACES FOR BUSINESS WEB APPLICATIONS

By Janko Jovanovic

BUSINESS WEB APPLICATION design is too often neglected. I see a lot of applications that don't meet the needs of either businesses or users and thus contribute to a loss of profit and poor user experience. It even happens that designers are not involved in the process of creating applications at all, putting all of the responsibility on the shoulders of developers.

This is a tough task for developers, who may have plenty of back-end and front-end development experience but limited knowledge of design. This results in unsatisfied customers, frustrated users, and failed projects.

This chapter covers the basics of user interface design for business Web applications. While one could apply many approaches, techniques, and principles to UI design in general, our focus here will be on *business* Web applications.

WEBSITES VS. WEB APPLICATIONS

Confusing Web applications and websites is easy, as is confusing user interface design and website design. But they are different both in essence and in many other ways.

A website is a collection of pages consisting mostly of static content, images, and video, with limited interactive functionality (i.e., except for the contact form and search functionality). The primary role of a website is to inform. Some websites use content management systems to render dynamic content, but their nature is still informational.

Web applications, on the other hand, are dynamic, interactive systems that help businesses perform business-critical tasks and that increase and measure their productivity. Thus, the primary role of a Web application is to perform a function that serves the user's needs according to defined business rules.

Web applications require a higher level of involvement and knowledge of the system on the part of the user. Users don't just stumble upon an application, do their work, and bounce off. They use it as a tool to perform critical tasks in their daily work. In the end, they cannot easily discontinue using the application and switch to another if they don't like how it's working, as is the case with websites.

DIFFERENT TYPES OF WEB APPLICATIONS

Business applications range in type from invoicing for freelancers to content management systems to document management systems to banking and financial systems.

We can distinguish between open and closed applications. Open systems are online applications that are easily accessible to anyone who opens an account. Users can access such applications via the Web and can open an account for free or by paying a fee.

A closed system (or line-of-business applications) is usually not accessible outside of the company that uses it. Closed systems can be considered "offline" applications (though many systems expose their functionality to business partners via either services or specialized interfaces). Such systems usually run on the company's local network and are available only to employees.

I don't know who coined it, but one term I especially like is weblication, which describes what a Web application is in general. This doesn't mean, though, that a Web application is a half-website half-application hybrid. It is far more complex than that.

FIRST, KNOW YOUR USERS

You've probably heard this advice a thousand times, and for good reason: A successful user interface focuses on users and their tasks. This is key, and too many developers have failed to create a good user experience. As Steve Krug said, "Developers like complexity; they enjoy discovering how something works."

When identifying your users, keep in mind that your clients are not the application's end users, and you are not a user. Although a client's management team will usually be interested in the project and try to influence decisions, remember that they won't be sitting in front of the computer several hours a day (unless the application is specifically for them).

HOW TO IDENTIFY USERS

Identifying users can be done using several techniques, such as user interviews, business stakeholder interviews, and the "shadowing" method of observation. Interviews can give you answers to questions about the users' knowledge of the system and computers in general, while shadowing can yield more detailed information about how users perform tasks and what errors they make. The method is called shadowing because the observer is like a shadow, watching and noting the steps a user takes.

If you don't have access to real users — either because you don't have permission or are designing an open application — you can use personas, a tool that helps identify users. Personas are a representation of real users, including their habits, goals, and motivations. Because certain information about users is often identified through business analysis, you can make use of it to create personas. If you are not familiar with the tool, a comic by Brad Colbow (`http://thinkvitamin.com/design/how-to-under-stand-your-users-with-personas/`) will help.

A persona represents real users, indicating their habits, goals, and motivation.

Task analysis helps identify what tasks users perform in their jobs, how they do them, how long they take, and what errors they make. Sometimes clients will be using an old version of an application while you are designing a replacement version. Make use of that old system and watch how users use it. Understanding their tasks and challenges will be easier that way.

Regardless of who your users are, in most cases, you will have to consider both novices and experts. Novice users should be enabled to learn as fast as possible, while expert users should be enabled to perform their tasks extremely efficiently. This may mean creating separate interfaces. But in many cases you will be able to accommodate both types of users in the same interface through various techniques, such as progressive disclosure.

Such research is usually done by business analysts. But if no one else is responsible for it, you should do it. Once you have the necessary information, you can begin with the design.

DESIGN PROCESS

You can follow one of any number of processes in designing the user interface. You might already have one. However, I would suggest that you consider the Agile approach. Why, you ask? Well, because for users (and clients), the user interface is the product. The bottom line is that they don't care about your sketches or fantastic back end or powerful server. All they want to see is the user interface.

So, how does Agile help? It helps through its key principle: the iterative approach. Each iteration consists of all of the phases defined by your process. This means that at the end of the first iteration, you will have a product that can be tested, a prototype.

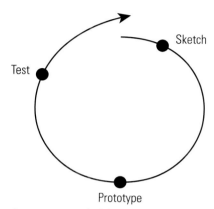

The iterative approach of the Agile design process

SKETCHING

Sketching is a powerful way to explore ideas. The goal is to arrive at the solution by sketching different concepts. Most sketches will be thrown out, but that is okay. As Bill Buxton says in his book, *Sketching User Experiences: Getting the Design Right and the Right Design,* sketches are fast to create and easy to dispose of, which is why they are so powerful.

Are sketches the same as wireframes? Well, the differences can be blurry, but I would say no. Wireframes don't capture rough ideas but rather develop them. Read a fantastic discussion on IxDA: *Sketching Before the Wireframes* (www.ixda.org/node/21817).

Once you get the "right" sketches, or at least the ones that you think are right, you can create more detailed wireframes or go straight to creating interactive prototypes.

PROTOTYPING

The next step in the process is to create prototypes that simulate the real application. A prototype can contain one or more features (or all of them), but it actually does nothing. It merely simulates the behavior of a real application, and users will feel that they are actually doing something. Prototypes may contain some functionality if needed (such as complex calculations).

Because the nature of a prototype done in HTML is temporary — its purpose, after all, is to test ideas — don't bother with the code; just make it work with minimal bugs. You will throw it away anyway. You can also use specialized prototyping software. Some people even prototype in PowerPoint.

TESTING

Prototypes are useless unless you test them. This is not rocket science. People like Jakob Nielsen and Steve Krug support so-called "discount usability testing," which is cheap and fast and yields valuable insight into your design decisions. You will use this information as the basis of another iteration of sketching, prototyping, and testing. Do this at least until major issues have been fixed. We all know that software projects are tight on time and budget, so to be more efficient, test early and test often.

One of the best resources for discount usability testing is a new book by Steve Krug, *Rocket Surgery Made Easy: The Do-It-Yourself Guide to Finding and Fixing Usability Problems.* Pick up a copy and read it.

DESIGN PRINCIPLES

There are many design principles, but there doesn't seem to be a general consensus on definitive ones. So, we'll go through design principles more informally, leaving out strict definitions.

NO ONE LIKES SURPRISES

Probably the key factors in a good UI are consistency and familiarity. A user interface should be consistent across all parts of the application, from navigation to color to terminology. This is known as internal consistency. But a user interface should also be consistent within its context, such as the operating system or other applications in its group or family. A typical example is the applications in the Microsoft Office family. This is called external consistency.

A good approach to consistency is to define user interface guidelines for each project or group of projects. These should guide the decisions you make for all of the details. This will not only maintain consistency but also serve as documentation to help team members better understand your decisions.

Consistent user interfaces have a shorter learning curve, because users will recognize parts of the system and be able to fall back on prior experience. But familiarity is sometimes confused with consistency. Familiar user interfaces draw on concepts from the users' previous experiences and use appropriate metaphors. Folders, for example, are a well-known metaphor for file organization, and they have replaced "directories," which were used previously in command-line operating systems. In short, speak the language of your users.

A common belief among business owners is that a great user interface should look like a Microsoft Office product, especially Outlook. I won't go into explaining how pointless this is. Rather, I will offer alternative advice: defend the user-centric approach, and explain why creating an application for employees, clients, and partners (i.e., their users) is so important.

All the same, most businesses are unique, as are their work processes. For example, two businesses from the same branch could have significantly different processes, forcing you to go beyond what is familiar and start to innovate. This part of the design process can be very interesting, although you have to be careful in how much you innovate.

USERS SHOULD BE ABLE TO BE EFFICIENT

Without a doubt, users should be able to be efficient when using business applications. This is what they are paid for, and this is what managers expect from the application. User interfaces should allow users to be efficient and should focus them on completing tasks in the easiest and fastest way.

But this is not always the case. There is an opinion, or at least practice, among developers that says the user interface should be as complex as the back-end system. No matter how ridiculous this sounds, the problem is real and could give you a headache. This is one reason why good communication and collaboration between developers is a must.

Users are efficient when they focus on a particular task. As mentioned, task analysis helps you identify tasks and determines how users perform them. If tasks are long, accelerate them by breaking them up into smaller units. You can also increase efficiency by providing keyboard support and shortcuts. Think how inefficient it is for a user to have to switch back and forth between mouse and keyboard. In some cases, you will be designing for users who are accustomed to working on command-line operating systems and the applications made for them. They will be keen to have keyboard support. One suggestion: when defining keyboard shortcuts, keep them consistent with those of common applications. For example, Ctrl + S should always be Save, and so on.

Google Docs Spreadsheet enables users to be efficient by providing keyboard shortcuts and context menus, as well as by taking advantage of users' familiarity with common desktop applications.

Reproduced from Google™

Efficiency can also be enhanced through personalization. Users who can personalize an environment will learn it faster and, more importantly, will be more confident using it. Personalization can be done in many ways: choosing widgets for the dashboard, defining shortcut options and favorites, changing the order of elements, etc.

Pay attention to accessibility. Although many assume that accessibility doesn't matter in Web applications, it certainly does. Treat the application as if it were a public website.

A Web application also has to be efficient in the speed with which it processes information. So, consider heavy interactions that result from partial renderings and AJAX requests.

HELP!

An interface should provide meaningful feedback that describes the state of the system to users. If an error occurs, users should be notified and informed of ways to recover. If an operation is in progress, users should be notified about the progress.

We can go even further and declare that user interfaces should prevent users from making errors. This principle, called forgiveness, can be followed with confirmation dialogs, undo options, forgiving formats, and more. Forgiveness makes it safe to explore the interface, decreases the learning curve and increases overall satisfaction.

Because of the complexity of business Web applications, you would also need to provide a comprehensive help system. This could be done with inline help, a support database, a knowledge base, and guided tours (which mix video, images, and text).

CAN'T GET NO SATISFACTION

Satisfaction is a subjective term that refers to how pleasant an interface is to use. Every design principle we have described here affects satisfaction. And a few more principles are worth mentioning.

Simplicity is a basic principle of UI design. The simpler a user interface, the easier it is to use. But keeping user interfaces for business applications simple is a challenge because the apps often have a lot of functionality.

The key is to balance functionality and simplicity. Restraint is one of the most efficient ways to achieve this balance, i.e., finding the simplest way to solve a problem.

Aesthetics, though subjective and somewhat arbitrary, play an important role in overall satisfaction. Users respond positively to pleasing user interfaces, sometimes even overlooking missing functionality. But you're not creating a work of art. One of the best articles to explain aesthetics is *In Defense of Eye Candy* (`www.alistapart.com/articles/indefense ofeyecandy/`).

In the end, users will be spending a lot of time in front of the business application, and no matter how usable, consistent, or forgiving the user interface is, satisfaction will be critical in determining how good it is.

ESSENTIAL COMPONENTS OF WEB APPLICATIONS

Every Web application is unique, but many of them contain common features. Although the implementation of any one of these features will vary, let's look at five of the most common ones.

WEB FORMS

Forms in general are important to Web applications. But as Luke Wroblewski says in his book *Web Form Design,* "No one likes filling in forms." That includes sign-up forms in business applications with dozens of fields.

Minimize the frustration of filling in forms. Provide inline validation and good feedback. Use defaults when possible. Don't forget about novice users. Use wizards to help them complete tasks faster, or use progressive disclosure to hide advanced (or infrequently used) features.

MASTER-DETAIL VIEWS

This is the technique of showing data in two separate but related views. One view shows a list of items, while the other shows details of the selected item. Master-detail views can be implemented across multiple pages or on individual ones.

DASHBOARDS

Many Web applications have dashboards. A dashboard is a view of the most important information needed to take action and make decisions. It is confined to a single page and is usually the starting point of an application. Dashboards are important because they enable users to access information and take action without having to dig through the application.

HEAVY USE OF TABLES

Because Web applications typically deal with large quantities of data that are easily accessible and sortable, tables are unavoidable. But this is not a bad thing. In fact, tables were made for this purpose. Don't confuse this with table-less layouts.

Effective tables are easily readable. So, in most cases you will need a meaningful header, an optimal number of columns, pagination, alternating row colors, proper column alignment, sorting and filtering capabilities, and much more.

Tables can also be interactive, meaning they are able to generate additional info and even modify the data they contain.

REPORTS

Most businesses work with some kind of reports. Printed reports are usually required, so pay attention to the design of reports. Printed (or exported) reports are usually simplified versions of online reports, optimized for monochrome printers.

DON'T FORGET UI DESIGN PATTERNS

We're so used to hearing and talking about UI design patterns that we sometimes forget about them! UI design patterns are helpful for designing user interfaces. The important thing is to consider them early on in the design process, ideally at the sketching stage.

Because patterns often solve common problems, the right pattern can facilitate the user's familiarity with an interface and increase the speed at which they learn it.

Master/ Detail

Column Browse

Search/ Results

Filter Dataset

Form

Palette/ Canvas

Dashboard

Spreadsheet

Wizard

Question & Answer

Parallel Panels

Interactive Model

Blank State

This screenshot is from the article "12 Standard Screen Patterns" (`http://designing`
`webinterfaces.com/designing-web-interfaces-12-screen-`
`patterns`), which reviews the most common screen patterns.

Copyright © 2009 Bill Scott & Theresa Neil. *Designing Web Interfaces* from O'Reilly Media

CASE STUDY: ONLINE BANKING APPLICATION

To take an example from the real world, I will briefly explain the process of designing the user interface for one small bank's online banking system. The team I worked with was hired to improve the system. The main reason for the redesign was that, according to management, "users complained and many stopped using it."

After only a couple of hours spent with actual users, the main problems were uncovered. Information about accounts and credit cards was buried in poor navigation. Understanding how much money users were spending and the state of their accounts and credit cards was also hard. The application, however, was obvious to bank employees; they were familiar with the terminology and could interpret the numbers in the application perfectly well.

Give the tight deadlines, we followed the process I have described, and we partially succeeded. Despite the short time, the major problems were so obvious that we clearly understood our main task and how to go about it. We created a dashboard that provided clear information on the state of all accounts and credit cards. With this new navigation, finding information became easier. Reports were easier to understand, and several new features were implemented.

Although we made only a few changes, the changes affected critical user tasks and resulted in significant improvements to the overall experience.

FINAL THOUGHTS

Designing user interfaces for business Web applications is a challenging job, full of compromise. You have to make compromises between client and user needs; business requirements and users; novice and expert users; functionality and simplicity.

It requires a solid understanding of users and their tasks, as well as of UI design principles and patterns. Despite the difficulties, the job is interesting, and you learn many new things on each project that influence the way you design websites.

Janko Jovanovic is a software engineer, blogger, and speaker focused on UI engineering. In his free time, he writes about UI engineering on his blog at JankoAtWarpSpeed.com.

6

PROGRESSIVE ENHANCEMENT AND STANDARDS DO NOT LIMIT WEB DESIGN

By Christian Heilmann

LATELY I HAVE been getting bored and annoyed with people getting up in arms against Web standards and the ideas of progressive enhancement, claiming that they hold us back from creating a rich, beautiful Web. There are also claims that these tools limit us from pushing the boundaries of what is possible with today's technologies.

The problem with claims such as these is that they are based on a misunderstanding of standards and progressive enhancement and — at least to me — on arrogance and ignorance about what our job on the Web is. The Web is out there for everybody and is a product and a medium like any other.

For example, I am a big film buff and love good movies. I understand, though, that in order to fund great movies we have to make money from terrible ones that appeal to the lowest common denominator or rehash ideas that were successful in the past.

The same applies to the Web: we need to shift our focus to what people use it for and what content should go on it, not how pretty we can make it or what cool technology we can apply. The beauty of Web technologies is that they can be used to build adaptive products. I cannot drive a tall truck through a low tunnel without damaging either the tunnel or the truck. Websites and apps, however, can easily make Transformers look clumsy — if we build them adaptively and collaboratively with a team of experts.

SHINY NEW TECHNOLOGIES VS. OUTDATED BEST PRACTICES

Dozens of case studies featuring CSS transformation and animation, and demos of the canvas element and HTML5 audio and video that "work only in the latest build of browser X," give us the illusion of a Web that could be so much richer and more beautiful. They also lead to claims that we are stalling because of the grumpy old people of the Web who claim that we have to follow rules and support outdated technology. Actually, none of this is about stalling: it is about maturing as an industry and embracing the adaptive nature of the Web. If you start a design and try to make it work all by yourself, then you have not understood the Web and its collaborative nature.

THE MESS THAT IS THE WEB

Good Web products are the result of successful collaboration. One-man armies with a limited view of the impact of putting something up on the Web lead to a steady stream of mediocre, unsecure, unmaintained, and hard-to-upgrade Web products. This includes all of those websites that look terrible but "do the job," the very big group of websites that are incredibly hard to use but still "communicate the brand's message," and the few that are stunningly beautiful at first glance and boring seconds later. Finding a truly usable, accessible, beautiful, maintained (and easy-to-maintain) website out there is almost impossible.

The reason is that experts tend to advocate for their field of expertise as being the most important one, instead of partnering with other experts and making both a better offer and subsequently a better product.

CREATING CELEBRITIES AND A PLACE WE WISH WE WERE AT

We look up to the "rock stars" of Web design, the people who "push the envelope," rather than praise teams that did an amazing job of delivering a great Web product in an existing but deficient infrastructure. Great technology always happens in environments where the designers or developers have full control over the content and technology and free reign to build something great.

This is pure escapism, because in the real world you never get any of this, unless you build websites for yourself.

It's frustrating, which is why instead of trying to change our work environment and make our mark as Web developers, we escape to Awesomeland, where everything is shiny and new and the client-side is really popping.

Returning from a conference at which you've glimpsed the future of CSS gives you the feeling of being part of something worthwhile. Less fulfilling is having to argue with your team to reserve time to write a plug-in that ensures your corporate CMS spits out clean, semantic HTML instead of a tag soup, or that at least allows you to add a class that gives you a style handle to work with. Now guess which in the long run will change the game? Probably both, but by fixing the underlying infrastructure, we enable cool new technologies to become relevant to the mass market.

We can build amazingly fast, low-riding cars that reach top speeds of 150 mph, but if the roads are full of potholes and crammed with cars, then they become little more than toys for rich people who own their own racetrack. The same applies to any design showcase in which texts are expected to be a certain length and products to be a fixed number, and where CSS knowledge is needed to make the website look right when you add a product.

This is not how people use the Web, and maintainers should not have to depend on experts to make changes to their websites. Websites change constantly; this is what makes them interesting and much more versatile than, say, print media.

HOLLYWOOD AND ADVERTISING TEACH US NOTHING

A lot of showcases hail movie websites for having the most feature richness and visual beauty. Well, try to find websites for older movies and you will see that most are 404 errors or "Not available any more" (for example, try to find out what exactly is the *Matrix*, and you'll be waiting a while). Is this the Web we should be putting our efforts into? Is this innovation? Or should we start to work as teams and add our unique talents to produce something better and more durable than what is merely pretty and what satisfies our own ideas of a great website? Isn't the main premise of Web design something that is available to millions of people worldwide and available longer than data stored on a cheap CD (whose lifespan is approximately 10 years, in case you were wondering)?

THE MYTH OF INNOVATING EXCLUSIVELY THROUGH TECHNOLOGY

Know what? In most cases, we are not innovating: this is not the revolution; it has been done before.

During the first browser wars, we were in exactly the same boat, and people were building things that worked only in certain browsers, and they claimed this was the future. I am sure you can guess which browser was the worst offender and why we're having a hard time getting rid of it now.

Yes, IE6. A lot of the websites in CSS3 showcases today, especially the animated ones, remind me painfully of the IE6 CSS expressions and page transition showcases of old. Did you know, for instance, that you could rotate text in IE5.5 with the matrix filter? The difference is that, back then computers were so slow that all of these effects looked bad; nowadays, on fast computers and shiny iPhones and iPads, they look much more impressive. While I am very happy that we don't use a hybrid technology that comes with a boatload of performance issues and a syntax that must have been defined in a feverish dream, I am also not convinced that the "CSS3" browser-forking that we do now to make websites work in this or that browser is future-proof either.

INNOVATION ISN'T ABOUT NEW TOYS

We generally tend to regard the use of the newest technology as "innovation." This is why you see old problems being solved with new technologies over and over again, even though they have already been solved. Pure-CSS menus, for example, were newer technology but were a step back in usability: you cannot delay the hiding of a menu and you cannot test if it will fit the screen before opening it.

For this, you need a technology that has two-way communication: you set something and then check that it worked. CSS does not have this checking mechanism; we are at the mercy of the browser doing it right. With Java-Script we have that option. We also have a sensible syntax in JavaScript;

whereas CSS, with all of its `-browser` extensions, is slowly but steadily turning into a syntactic nightmare.

CSS has developed some great defensive features: for example, media queries, which allow different designs to be served to different screen sizes automatically, are wonderful. However, does CSS need all of these features, and should we have to wait for universal browser support, or would it make more sense to use JavaScript now in conjunction with CSS to achieve the same effect? A good CSS designer and someone with rudimentary knowledge of JavaScript libraries are all it takes. But oh no, why share the fame when we can do it with CSS3 alone?

Innovation is not about using the newest technology exclusively. Innovation also happens when you combine existing tools and make good use of them. Flints were great as spearheads for killing each other or skinning animals. Hitting them with another rock or against each other all of a sudden gave us fire. No one showed up with a lighter to teach people how it works. Instead, we analyzed what we had and put it to good use. And guess what? Flints don't need fuel either.

THE CORPORATE SPIN ON INNOVATION, AND ITS CONSEQUENCES

The other thing we should never forget is that every time we innovate, some people will one way or another sell these ideas to corporate IT half a year later. Most of the time, the innovation is sold as part of a bigger software package: "Oh yeah, our CMS package Overpriced-And-Underspec'ed-otron now supports AJAX… in multiple colors!" Sadly, this also happens to be the only time when the innovation will have a real impact on the mass market.

If we really think that large corporations or end users care about what we do, we're fooling ourselves. In the end, software and the Internet exist to solve the problems of people. And sadly, the people deciding on the best solutions are not us but rather those who only go for what's cheapest and seemingly the most secure.

A large company that offers a corporation its software package at a fixed price, promising to solve all of the issues plaguing the corporation's daily workflow and to train the people who work with the software are selling much more easily than us with our "We will help you understand the Web and make it easier for your employees to be more effective" pitch. Which sounds like more work for an already overloaded IT decision-maker?

THE STOCKHOLM SYNDROME OF BAD INTERFACES

This breeds a lot of ordinary interfaces on the Web that are painful to use and terrible to look at. The amazing thing, though, is that people love to use them. This is what they learned in corporate training, and these are the products supported and endorsed by the company.

Memorizing five convoluted steps and mechanically going through them every time is easier than finding the time to learn new things. There is a comfort in knowing how to get the results you are asked to get in a predicable way if you really don't want to use something to begin with.

If you don't want to be one of the people who builds the Web, then every change becomes an annoyance — upgrading being one of them.

This is why we have outdated set-ups: not because of evil companies that refuse to embrace new technologies, but rather because people couldn't be bothered to upgrade because no perceptive gain comes from it.

Instead of targeting the people who really prevent the Web from evolving and giving them something to consider as a great gain, we stay in our comfort zone, talking to each other about pushing the envelope and suffering from the wider market not caring.

Want to drive the Web forward? Find a way to disrupt the five-year upgrade cycle of corporate environments. Whenever you talk to the leading lights of Web design about this, you get an answer like, "This is a battle we can't win."

THIS IS NOT ABOUT TECHNOLOGY OR DESIGN

In the end, we deliver products. We are passionate about the Web, and we want to push it forward. The problem is that we stay in our comfort zone rather than expand our knowledge:

- Designers want to push the envelope toward richer interaction and more beautiful designs with rich typography.
- UX people want to make it darned easy for people to achieve their goals; and if a pattern works well on the desktop, it should also work well on the Web.

- Engineers push for speed, with "best practices on performance" that are relevant to search result pages and Web apps like Gmail but not so much to content-heavy websites.
- Other engineers want to build the most versatile and flexible platform ever so that people can use it without ever having to bother the engineers again (because they would have already moved on to solving other problems).
- Mobile enthusiasts start to abandon the idea of Web technologies as the way forward because the technologies are too limited and too far removed from the capabilities of the platform.

A lot of these are mutually exclusive, and the last point is especially not true and only happens because we as Web developers forgot the nature of the Web: a technology stack that adapts to the needs of the end user — data that has a clever morphing interface that gives each use case the interface it needs. That the Web began as a text platform and evolved into a rich media system is great; that we want to replace one with the other is just plain wrong or at least very premature.

WHERE IS THE BEAUTY OF THE WEB?

Here is the real beauty of Web design: adaptability; interfaces that adapt to the needs of the user independent of their technology or physical ability. We forgot this for a few reasons:

- *We're control freaks:* We like to control what we do and are afraid of chaos and people messing with our products. Sure, we love to be disruptive and break conventions, but only when we can choose the font-face and colors.
- *We're bitter:* For years, we worked tirelessly to make the Web better and more beautiful, and our clients hardly ever cared. We were constantly promised to be allowed to build something amazing, and then our budgets were cut or we had to move on to the next project before adding that last little element that would have made it awesome.
- *Cheap thrills:* It is easy to draw praise for "thinking outside the box" by telling people that progressive enhancement is dead or that IE6 should no longer be supported or that everyone you know has a 1920-pixel resolution. You get applauded, and people look up to you because this is exactly what they want to tell their boss every day. But does it help us? Or are we getting praise by escaping to our own world?

- *Frustration about the end product:* We are hardly ever able to look at a live product and say, "This is cool and looks exactly as we planned." Even worse, after a year of maintenance, we are lucky even to be able to recognize it as our work. Portfolios are outdated as soon as we put them up (I know because I am hiring people right now and cannot assess their quality of work that way).

- *Arrogance and ignorance:* Our market, our HR practices, and even our job boards clearly distinguish between designers and developers. Instead of challenging this and acknowledging "Web developers" who grasp both the user experience and the command line, we are content to stay in our own silos.

A developer who claims not to need design input is as useless as a designer who doesn't care about the technical implementation of their design. We should encourage each other to build the best products through collaboration, and not regard each other as show-stoppers or whiners who always want it their way.

TO RECAP: OUR ISSUES

So here are the issues you have to face as someone who wants to build great Web products:

- *The technology stack you're asked to support is unknown.* You can fool yourself into believing that everyone out there is as happy to upgrade and chase after the newest technology, but doing it just shows that it's been a while since you had to deliver a real project.

- *Outdated technology is here to stay.* People either are not allowed to upgrade or simply don't care. When I watch TV, I don't want to know how its internals work, and a lot of Web users think this way, too.

- *Your work will be butchered.* The website you plan to build will be changed over the course of the project (e.g. the client runs out of money, which always happens), and what you do manage to get out will be changed over the years to something you never intended to build.

- *You can't know everything.* When you put a product on the Web, you need to make it do the following: work for humans, look pleasing, perform well, be secure, be extensible, have the option to be localized to different markets and languages, be easy to change and adapt, and be cheap to run and migrate to another environment. If you can do all of that, please send me your CV… on second thought, don't, because I'm sure you'll be a poor team player.

- *You can't rely on solutions standing the test of time.* A lot of "great tricks" and "best practices" come with a massive price that gets paid a few months down the line. Many solutions that were once the bee's knees are now considered bad practice (table layouts, for example, were at one time the bulletproof solution for flaky CSS layouts).

All of this points to a truth that I learned long ago: following standards and enhancing progressively means building stuff that will not come back to haunt you down the line.

WHY STANDARDS MATTER, AND WHAT "FOLLOWING STANDARDS" MEANS

Working toward a standard means two things: making it easy for others to build on your work, and having a fixed point to start from. The thing about standards in any professional environment is that they work. They might not be the best or most elegant solution, but by sticking to them you are at least delivering a workable solution. This is why we standardized screws and print sizes and also why one can find boilerplate contracts around.

Products built somewhere else by someone unknown will still be maintainable if the developers followed a standard — even if the product lacks documentation. I can still put my old Lego cars together from the parts even though I lost the booklets. If I had sawed off parts of the Legos or bent them to make them prettier, I wouldn't be able to do that.

By following standards, you are signing an agreement with the people who take over from you, saying: no big surprises ahead — I'm a professional.

That said, don't look at standards as a "by any means necessary" proposition. Adding ARIA roles to your HTML right now, for example, would make the W3C validator complain, but the roles allow people to quickly navigate your document without your having to write custom keyboard navigation with "skip" links.

PROGRESSIVE ENHANCEMENT WORKS

Progressive enhancement is not about supporting old platforms: anyone who says this totally misunderstands the concept. Progressive enhancement means one thing: delivering what can be supported to the right platform. This means the following:

- *Including everything that is absolutely necessary for the comprehension and functionality of the website in HTML.* Not static HTML, mind you, but HTML rendered by a well-written back end that gets the data via an API.
- *Keeping the look and feel as much in CSS as possible.* If you need a few HTML elements to achieve a certain look, that is not an issue whatsoever. This is actually why we have elements like SPAN and DIV. You will find standards zealots who frown upon every extra DIV on the page. Tell those people to chill out.
- *Enhancing the behavior of the product with a richer interactive layer.* This could be CSS for hovers, transitions, and animations, or JavaScript, or Flash, or Silverlight… heck, throw in Java applets if you want. As long as you add them only when appropriate, you're not doing anything wrong.

A great pragmatic example of progressive enhancement in action is SWFObject and SoundManager. Instead of putting a Flash movie into the document and hoping it works, put a download link to the audio or video in the document, add a JavaScript, and let the script do the rest. It checks whether Flash is supported by the browser and creates the right markup for the given browser to embed the audio or video only when it is able to be played. Everyone gets to see the movie or hear the sound, but only those browsers that can support a player will show one.

The main test of good progressive enhancement is this: are you offering functionality that you are not sure will work? If not, then congratulations: you have built a great Web product. Testing before implementation is as obvious as checking the depth of a lake before jumping in. There is no magic to it.

One big benefit of progressive enhancement that is often forgotten is that by separating the different tasks of a Web product into different technologies, you are able to segment the workflow and assign each part to a different team.

A progressively enhanced product can be built in parallel by the back-end team, the front-end developers, and the UX and design team. If you start with the design and try to trace your way back, you aren't working together but rather throwing work over a wall and probably causing existing code to be changed or even totally re-architected. To save time, enhance progressively and measure twice, cut once.

The product cycle should begin with a definition of basic functionality; once this is agreed on, all groups can work in parallel and reconvene at later stages in an iterative fashion and make the product a bit better every time. This also means that if there is an emergency and funding gets canned, you can at least deliver a working product. Agile, isn't it?

BEST PRACTICES COME FROM APPLICATION AND ITERATIVE IMPROVEMENT

To improve our entire market, we have to stop advertising everything we do as a "best practice." Best practices should come from real products built by real teams for real clients, with all of the annoyances and problems they bring. Test cases that cover all "current" browsers are nice, but many more things can throw a spanner in the works when we build real products.

So, if you work at a company and managed to implement some cool new technology in an existing product or have stories to tell about how shifting to a CSS layout saved your client thousands of dollars, please write about those. We need tangible stories to tell clients, not tales of a bright future.

Furthermore, scrutinize every "best practice" you find in your own environment: does it really deliver on its promise? Does something need to be added to make it work in the "real world"?

TOGETHER WE CAN DO THIS

The last thing I want to bring up here is that I am tired of the debate about developer vs. designer vs. project manager. As listed above, real Web projects require a lot of different skill sets, and you would be hard pressed either to find someone who possesses all of them or to find the time to learn them all yourself and stay up to date.

It is all about teamwork, trust, delegation, and communication. If we stay cooped up in our respective ivory towers and complain that we can't work with the other groups, while pretending that we could do their jobs anyway if only people would upgrade their browsers, then we shouldn't be surprised that we don't get the time and opportunity to own and deliver a real Web product, as opposed to some piece of software with a Web interface.

Christian Heilmann is an international Developer Evangelist working for the Yahoo Developer Network in the lovely town of London, England.

COLOR THEORY FOR PROFESSIONAL DESIGNERS

By Cameron Chapman

COLOR IN DESIGN is very subjective. What evokes one reaction in one person may evoke a very different reaction in someone else. Sometimes this is due to personal preference, and other times due to cultural background. Color theory is a science in itself. Studying how colors affect different people, either individually or as a group, is something some people build their careers on. And there's a lot to it.

Something as simple as changing the hue or saturation of a color can evoke a completely different feeling. Cultural differences mean that something that's happy and uplifting in one country can be depressing in another.

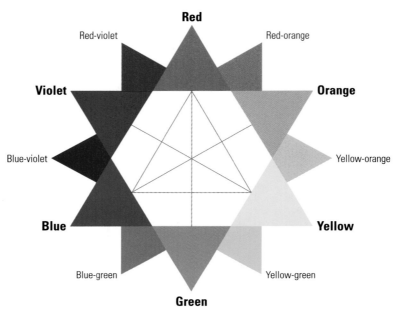

Web designers need a good understanding of the emotional impact of color.

WARM COLORS

Warm colors include red, orange, and yellow and variations of the three. These are the colors of fire, fall leaves, and sunsets and sunrises, and they are generally energizing, passionate, and positive.

Warm colors evoke energy and passion.

Red and yellow are both primary colors, with orange falling in the middle, which means warm colors are all truly warm and aren't created by combining a warm color with a cool color. Use warm colors in your designs to reflect passion, happiness, enthusiasm, and energy.

RED (PRIMARY COLOR)

Red is a hot color. It's associated with fire, violence, and warfare. It's also associated with love and passion. In history, it has been associated with both the devil and Cupid. Red can actually have a physical effect on people, raising blood pressure and respiration rate. It has been shown to enhance human metabolism, too.

Red is hot and passionate, but can be overpowering.

Red can be associated with anger, but it is also associated with status (think of the red carpet at awards shows and celebrity events). Red also indicates danger (which is the reason stop lights and signs are red and why most warning labels are red).

Outside the western world, red has different associations. For example, in China, red is the color of prosperity and happiness. It can also be used to attract good luck. In other eastern cultures, red is worn by brides on their wedding day. In South Africa, though, red is the color of mourning. Red is also associated with communism. Red has become the color associated with AIDS awareness in Africa due to the popularity of the RED campaign.

In design, red can be a powerful accent color. It can have an overwhelming effect if used too much in designs, especially in its purest form. It's a great color to convey power or passion in a design. Red can be versatile, though, with brighter shades being energetic and darker shades evoking power and elegance.

ORANGE (SECONDARY COLOR)

Orange is a vibrant and energetic color. In its muted forms, it is associated with Earth and the autumn season. Because of its association with the changing seasons, orange can represent change and movement in general.

Orange is vibrant and evokes health and vitality.

Because orange is also a fruit, it can be associated with health and vitality. In designs, orange commands attention without being as overpowering as red. It's often considered more friendly and inviting, and less in-your-face.

YELLOW (PRIMARY COLOR)

Yellow is often considered the brightest and most energizing of the warm colors. It is associated with happiness and sunshine. But yellow can also be associated with deceit and cowardice (calling someone yellow is to call them a coward).

Yellow is associated with happiness and energy, but also deceit.

Yellow is also associated with hope, as can be seen in countries where yellow ribbons are worn by families that have loved ones at war. Yellow is also associated with danger, though not as strongly as red. In some countries, yellow has very different connotations. In Egypt, for example, yellow is for mourning. In Japan it represents courage, and in India it's a color for merchants.

In your designs, bright yellow can lend a sense of happiness and cheerfulness. Softer yellows are commonly used as a gender-neutral color for babies (rather than blue or pink) and young children. Light yellows also give more of a feeling of calm and happiness than bright yellows. Dark yellows and gold-hued yellows can look antique and be used in designs where a sense of permanence is desired.

COOL COLORS

Cool colors include green, blue, and purple, and they are often more subdued than warm colors. They are the colors of night, water, and nature and are usually calming, relaxing and somewhat reserved.

Cool colors provide a sense of calm.

Blue is the only primary color in the cool spectrum, which means that the other colors are created by combining blue with a warm color (yellow for green and red for purple). Greens take on some of the attributes of yellow, and purple takes on some of the attributes of red. Use cool colors in your designs to give a sense of calm or professionalism.

GREEN (SECONDARY COLOR)

Green is a down to earth color. It represents new beginnings and growth. It also signifies renewal and abundance. Alternatively, green can represent envy, jealousy, or a lack of experience.

Green combines the calming effect of blue with the energy of yellow.

Green has many of the same calming attributes as blue, but it also carries some of the energy of yellow. In design, green can have a balancing and harmonizing effect, and it is stable. It's appropriate for designs related to wealth, stability, renewal, and nature. Brighter greens are energizing and vibrant, while olive greens represent the natural world. Dark greens are the most stable and representative of affluence.

BLUE (PRIMARY COLOR)

Blue is often associated with sadness in the English language. Blue is also used extensively to represent calmness and responsibility. Light blues can be refreshing and friendly. Dark blues are stronger and more reliable. Blue is also associated with peace and has spiritual and religious connotations in many cultures and traditions (for example, the Virgin Mary is generally depicted wearing a blue robe).

Various shade and hues of blue can evoke a range of emotions.

The significance of blue depends largely on its shade and hue. The shade of blue you select will have a huge impact on how your design is perceived. Light blues are often relaxing and calming. Bright blues can be energizing and refreshing. Dark blues are excellent for corporate websites and websites where strength and reliability are important.

PURPLE (SECONDARY COLOR)

Purple has long been associated with royalty. It's a combination of red and blue and takes on attributes of both. It is associated with creativity and imagination, too.

Purple is associated with wealth and royalty.

In Thailand, purple is the color of mourning for widows. Dark purples are traditionally associated with wealth and royalty, while lighter purples (like lavender) are considered more romantic.

In design, dark purples give a sense wealth and luxury. Light purples are softer and associated with spring and romance.

NEUTRALS

Neutral colors often serve as a backdrop in design. They're commonly combined with brighter accent colors. But they can also be used on their own and make for very sophisticated layouts. Surrounding colors affect the meaning of neutral colors much more than warm and cool colors.

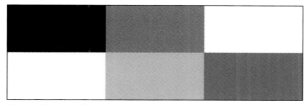

Neutral colors can add sophistication to a design.

BLACK

Black is the strongest of the neutral colors. On the positive side, it's associated with power, elegance, and formality. On the negative side, it is associated with evil, death, and mystery. Black is the traditional color of mourning in many Western countries. It's also associated with rebellion in some cultures and is tied to Halloween and the occult.

Black has both positive and negative connotations.

Black is commonly used in edgy designs, as well as in elegant designs. It can be either conservative or modern, traditional or unconventional, depending on the colors it's combined with. In design, black is commonly used for typography and other functional elements because of its neutrality. Black conveys a sense of sophistication and mystery.

WHITE

White is at the opposite end of the spectrum, but like black, it works well with just about any other color. White is often associated with purity, cleanliness, and virtue. In the West, white is commonly worn by brides on their wedding day. It's also associated with the health care industry, especially doctors, nurses, and dentists. White is associated with goodness: angels are often depicted in white dress.

White is associated with purity and cleanliness.

In design, white is often used as a neutral backdrop to give other colors a louder voice. It conveys cleanliness and simplicity and is popular in minimalist designs. White is also used to represent either winter or summer, in conjunction with the design motifs and colors around it.

GRAY

Gray is a neutral color, generally considered to be on the cool end of the spectrum. It can be considered moody or depressing. Light grays can be used in place of white in some designs, and dark grays can be used in place of black.

Gray can be depressing, but is also considered modern and sophisticated.

Gray is generally conservative and formal but can also be modern. It is sometimes considered a color of mourning. It's commonly used in corporate designs, where formality and professionalism are needed. It can be a sophisticated color. Pure grays are shades of black, though other grays may have blue or brown hues mixed in. In design, gray backgrounds are very common, as is gray typography.

BROWN

Brown is associated with earth, wood, and stone. It's a completely natural color and a warm neutral. Brown can be associated with dependability and reliability, with steadfastness and with earthiness. It can also be considered dull.

Brown may represent natural materials — stone, wood, and earth.

In design, brown is commonly used as a background color. It's also seen in wood textures and sometimes in stone textures. It gives a feeling of warmth and wholesomeness to a design. It's sometimes used in its darkest forms as a replacement for black, in either backgrounds or typography.

BEIGE AND TAN

Beige is somewhat unique in the color spectrum, because it can take on cool or warm tones depending on the colors around it. It has the warmth of brown and the coolness of white and, like brown, is sometimes seen as dull. It's a conservative color in most instances and is usually reserved for backgrounds. It also symbolizes piety.

Beige can be cool or warm, depending on surrounding colors.

Beige is generally used for backgrounds, often ones with a paper texture. It takes on characteristics of the colors around it, minimizing its effect on the overall design.

CREAM AND IVORY

Ivory and cream are sophisticated colors, with some of the warmth of brown and a lot of the coolness of white. They're generally quiet and often evoke a sense of history. Ivory is a calm color, with some of the pureness associated with white, but a bit warmer.

Ivory and cream are quiet and calming.

In design, ivory lends elegance and a sense of calm. When combined with earthy colors like peach or brown, it can take on an earthy quality. It can also be used to lighten darker colors, without the stark contrast of white.

IN BRIEF

While the information presented here might seem just a bit overwhelming, color theory is as much about the feeling a particular shade evokes as anything else. But here's a quick reference guide for the common meanings of the colors discussed previously:

Red	Passion, love, anger
Orange	Energy, happiness, vitality
Yellow	Happiness, hope, deceit
Green	New beginnings, abundance, nature
Blue	Calmness, responsibility, sadness
Purple	Creativity, royalty, wealth

Black	Mystery, elegance, evil
Gray	Moody, conservative, formal
White	Purity, cleanliness, virtue
Brown	Natural, wholesome, dependable
Tan or Beige	Conservative, pious, dull
Cream or Ivory	Calm, elegant, pure

TRADITIONAL COLOR SCHEME TYPES

There are a number of color scheme standards, which make creating new schemes easier, especially for beginners. The following sections describe the traditional schemes, with a few examples of each.

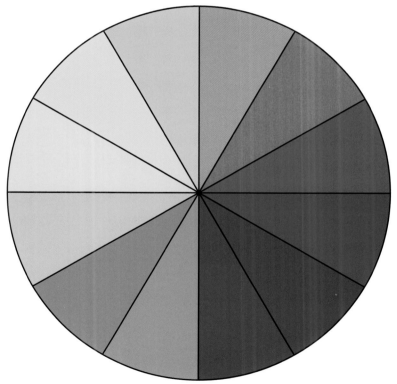

The basic 12-spoke color wheel is an important tool in creating color schemes.

MONOCHROMATIC

Monochromatic color schemes are made up of different tones, shades, and tints of a particular hue. These are the simplest color schemes to create, because they're all of the same hue, making it hard to create a jarring or ugly scheme (though that is still possible).

Here are three examples of monochrome color schemes. For the most part, the first color (from left to right) would be used for headlines. The second would be used for body text or possibly the background. The third color would be used for the background (or for the body text if the second color was used as the background). And the last two colors would be used as accents or in graphics.

Blue monochrome scheme

Berry monochrome scheme

Gold monochrome scheme

ANALOGOUS

Analogous color schemes are the next easiest to create. Analogous schemes consist of three colors that lie next to each other on the 12-spoke color wheel. Generally, analogous color schemes all have the same chroma level, but by using tones, shades, and tints we add interest and adapt the schemes to our needs.

This is a traditional analogous color scheme, and while it's visually appealing, there isn't enough contrast between the colors for an effective website design.

Here's a color scheme with the same hues as the one above, but with the chroma adjusted to give more variety. It's now much more suitable for use on a website.

Another example of a traditional analogous scheme.

This scheme modifies the previous one for use on a website.

COMPLEMENTARY

Complementary schemes are created by combining colors from opposite sides of the color wheel. In their most basic form, these schemes consist of only two colors but can be easily expanded using tones, tints, and shades. A word of warning, though: using colors that are exact opposites with the same chroma and/or value right next to each other can be jarring (they'll seem to vibrate along their border in extreme cases). Avoid this, either by leaving white space between them or by adding a transitional color between them.

A wide range of tints, shades, and tones makes this a versatile color scheme.

Another complementary color scheme with a wide range of chromas. Don't forget that beige and brown are really tints and shades of orange.

SPLIT COMPLEMENTARY

Split complementary schemes are almost as easy to use as complementary schemes. Here, instead of using opposite colors, you would use colors on either side of the hue that is opposite to your base hue.

A scheme in which yellow-green is the base hue. In this scheme, having enough difference in chroma and value between the colors you select is important.

Another palette with a wide range of chromas.

TRIADIC

Triadic schemes are made up of hues that are equally spaced around the 12-spoke color wheel. These make for more vibrant color schemes.

Using a very pale or dark version of one color in the triad, along with two shades, tones, or tints of the other two colors, makes the single color work almost as a neutral.

Alternatively, pairing one very bright hue with muted hues makes the bright one stand out more.

DOUBLE-COMPLEMENTARY (TETRADIC)

Tetradic color schemes are probably the most difficult to pull off.

A rather unimpressive scheme. The best tetradic schemes use one color as the primary color and the others as accents.

Tetradic color schemes with similar chromas and values work well. Just add a neutral (such as dark gray or black) for text and accents.

It works just as well for darker color schemes.

CUSTOM

Custom color schemes are the hardest to create. By not following the predefined schemes discussed above, you're abandoning any formal rules. Keep in mind things like chroma, value, and saturation when creating custom color schemes.

The colors here all have similar chroma and saturation levels.

Again, using colors with similar chroma and saturation is effective and creates a sense of cohesion.

Using one color with a high chroma among other colors with lower chromas is another effective method (the higher-chroma color serves as an accent).

CREATING A COLOR SCHEME

Creating your own color schemes can be a bit intimidating. But it's not as complicated as many people think. And you can employ quite a few tricks to create great color palettes right from the start.

We've gone over the different types of color schemes. Now, let's try creating a few of our own. Plenty of tools are online that will help you create a color scheme, but for now we'll just use Photoshop.

Let's break away from the types already mentioned and create some custom schemes. While knowing how colors interact and how traditional schemes are created is important, for most design projects you'll likely create schemes that don't adhere strictly to any predefined patterns.

So, for our purposes here, we'll create a set of three color schemes for two different websites. Our hypothetical clients are a modern architecture design blog and a high-end women's clothing retailer that specializes in Victorian-influenced apparel.

We'll start with a basic monochromatic scheme, just to get a feel for it. While traditional color schemes aren't used as much in design, monochromatic color schemes are the exception. You'll likely find yourself using monochromatic schemes on a fairly regular basis.

For our apparel store, here's a traditional monochromatic scheme, with white added as a neutral.

Basic monochromatic scheme for the apparel store

For our design blog, we've gone with a color scheme made up of shades and tints of gray.

Monochromatic scheme for the design blog

Next is almost an analogous color scheme, but we've left out one color. It's made up of shades of purple and reddish-purple. These two colors fall next to each other on the color wheel and work well together, especially when given different values and saturation levels.

Adding purple shades to the scheme

Adding a couple of shades of red to this gray color scheme adds a lot of visual interest and the potential to highlight certain parts of your design.

Adding red increases visual interest.

For the next scheme, we've gotten rid of the purple hues and switched to a burgundy. Again, this is next to the reddish-purple on the color wheel. We've also added a very pale yellow tone, which sits opposite purple on the color wheel. This serves as our neutral and looks more like an off-white compared to our other hues.

Using burgundy

The next color scheme at first glance looks like another standard gray and red palette. However, grays are actually tones of blue. Blue and red make up two thirds of a tetradic color scheme, but they work just fine together without yellow, especially when the red is pure and the blue is toned down to the point of almost being gray.

Adding some blue to the gray tones

WHY SHADES, TONES, AND TINTS ARE IMPORTANT

As you can see from the color schemes above, using tints, tones, and shades in your color schemes is vital. Pure hues all have similar values and saturation levels. This leads to color schemes that are overwhelming and boring at the same time.

When you mix in tones, shades, and tints, you expand the basic 12-spoke color wheel to an infinite number of possible colors. One of the simplest ways to create a professional-looking scheme is to take a few tones, tints, and shades of a given color (avoiding the pure hue), and then add another pure (or close to pure) hue that is at least three spaces away on the color wheel (i.e. that's part of a tetradic, triadic or split-complementary scheme) as an accent color. This adds visual interest while still retaining a sense of balance.

ADDING IN NEUTRALS

Neutrals are another important part of color schemes. Gray, black, white, brown, tan, and off-white are generally considered neutral. Browns, tans, and off-whites tend to make color schemes warmer (because they're really just tones, shades, and tints of orange and yellow). Gray takes on a warm or cool feel depending on the surrounding colors. Black and white also look either warm or cool depending on the surrounding colors.

Using a bright color to change the impact of a neutral scheme

Black and white are the easiest neutrals to add to just about any color scheme. To add a bit more visual interest, though, consider using a very light or very dark shade of gray instead.

Adding browns, tans, and off-white hues is a bit trickier, but with practice you'll find it gets easier. For browns, consider using a very dark chocolate brown in place of black. A pale off-white can be used instead of white or light gray in many cases. And tan can be used in place of gray (create a tone by adding some gray to make it even easier).

THE EASIEST COLOR SCHEMES

We've touched on this already: adding a bright accent color to an otherwise neutral palette is one of the easiest color schemes to create. It's also one of the most striking. If you're unsure of your skill in creating custom schemes, start out with these types of palettes.

Here are a few examples to give you an idea.

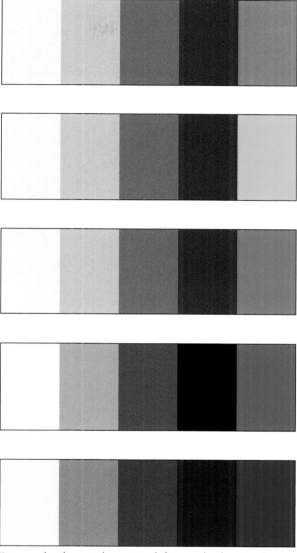

You can see here how using browns instead of grays makes the entire scheme warmer, even with the blue accent color.

You can use tones of any color instead of gray or brown in this type of scheme; just keep it close to the gray end of the spectrum for the most foolproof results. As a general rule, cool grays and pure grays are best for modern designs. For traditional designs, warmer grays and browns work better.

HOW MANY COLORS?

You'll notice that throughout this chapter we've used color schemes with five different colors. Five is a good number: it gives plenty of options for illustrating the concepts discussed here and it is a workable number in a design. But feel free to use more or fewer colors in your own schemes.

A lot of websites might have only three colors. Others only two. And some might have eight or ten (which is a lot trickier). Experiment, and use as many or few colors as you need. But you may want to start with a palette of five, and then add or subtract as you see fit and as you progress.

The easiest way to add a color is to start with a predefined traditional color scheme and go from there. This gives you at lease a bit of direction as far as which other colors to consider.

CONCLUSION

We've really only touched on color theory in this chapter. Specialists out there have spent literally years refining their ability to choose the appropriate colors for the situation.

The best way to learn how to create beautiful color schemes is to practice. Create a scheme every day. You can either start with automated tools or just fire up Photoshop and begin. If you come across a particularly beautiful or striking color, try creating a scheme around it.

Take advantage of one of the many websites out there that let you upload your color schemes and organize them for later reference. They make your library more practical and easier to use in future.

Cameron Chapman is a professional Web and graphic designer with over six years of experience. She writes for a number of blogs, including her own, Cameron Chapman On Writing. She's also the author of Internet Famous: A Practical Guide to Becoming an Online Celebrity.

IS JOHN THE CLIENT DENSE, OR ARE YOU FAILING HIM?

By Paul Boag

MEET JOHN THE client. John runs a reasonably large website. He is a marketer who considers himself smart, articulate, and professional. That said, he doesn't know much about Web design, and so he needs your help. John comes to you with a clear set of business objectives and asks for a quote. But what happens next leaves John confused, frustrated, and extremely unhappy.

EXPLAIN WHY YOU ARE ASKING ABOUT MONEY

Before giving John his quote, you ask a little more about the project. After chatting for a few minutes, you ask him about his budget. A fair question, you think. After all, you could approach the project in so many ways.

Without knowing the budget, knowing where to begin is impossible. In your mind, building a website is like building a house. Without knowing the budget, you can't possibly know how many rooms the client can afford or what materials you should use to build.

John, on the other hand, is instantly suspicious. Why would you want to know about his budget? The only reason he can think of is that you want to make sure you don't charge him less than what he is willing to give. Besides, he doesn't really know his budget. How the heck is he supposed to know how much a website costs?

John leaves, determined to find a Web designer who doesn't want to take advantage of him. Fortunately for you, all of the other designers he speaks with also neglect to explain why they need to know about his budget, and so you manage to win the project after all.

JUSTIFY YOUR RECOMMENDATIONS IN LANGUAGE JOHN CAN UNDERSTAND

Once you have won the job, you arrange a kick-off meeting to nail down the specifications. However, John instantly regrets his decision to hire you because his worst fears have been confirmed. In his eyes, you are all of a sudden trying to squeeze more money out of him as you blab on about the importance of usability and accessibility. John doesn't care about disabled users. He doesn't expect disabled users to visit his website anyway.

And as for usability, surely the job of the Web designer is to make the website usable. Why do we need expensive usability testing? He is pretty certain that usability testing involves expensive things like cameras, labs, and two-way mirrors. You thought you had explained these issues clearly. You spoke of WCAG 2, and you mentioned Jakob Nielsen. You are beginning to wonder if John is a bit thick.

Perhaps if you had talked about accessibility in terms of assessing search engine rankings and testing usability as a way to increase conversion, then John might have listened. As it is, John puts his foot down and refuses to pay for any of these "unnecessary extras."

INCLUDE JOHN IN THE PROCESS

You walk away from the kick-off meeting pleased to have a signed contract. But that feeling in the pit of your stomach tells you that this might be another one of those projects. Regardless, you try to be optimistic, and you dive into the design process. Almost immediately, you get a phone call from John asking if there is anything for him to see. You explain that it is still early in the process and that you are not ready to present anything. John sounds disappointed but resigned.

A short while later, you are ready to present the design to John. You are pleased with the result. It took you a lot more time than you had budgeted for, but it was worth it. The final design is extremely easy to use and will make for a great portfolio piece.

When John sees the design, he is horrified. From his perspective, you have entirely missed the point. The design clashes with his offline marketing materials and doesn't hit the right selling points. Also, he is convinced that his suppliers will hate it and, although they are not his end users, their opinion matters.

After a tense conference call, you feel demoralized but have struck a compromise that hopefully will make John happy. You wonder in hindsight whether showing John some of your initial ideas and sketches would have been better. Perhaps you should have presented a wireframe first.

EDUCATE JOHN ABOUT DESIGN

After much agonizing and compromise, you are once again ready to present to John. John is much happier with the new design and feels it is heading in the right direction. However, he does have some concerns. For starters, he has to scroll to see most of the content, and yet white space takes up either side of the design. He tells you to move key content into this wasted space. Also, as he thinks about his young male target audience, he realizes that the color scheme is too effeminate, so he tells you to change it to blue.

While John feels somewhat happier, you feel crushed. You feel as though he is trying to do the job for you. The instructions to move this there and change this color to that makes you feel like you have been reduced to pushing pixels.

By this point, you are sure the client is dim, and now you just want him to sign off on a design. At no stage do you think to ask John why he is requesting these changes. Perhaps if you had appreciated his thinking, you could have explained concepts such as screen resolution and suggested an alternative to corporate blue, which is so over-used on the Web. Instead, you wash your hands of the design and just give John what he wants.

COMMUNICATE WITH JOHN REGULARLY

Now that the design is complete, you turn your attention to building it. John certainly won't care about your code. Now you can finally do things right.

It's a big job and takes a lot of time. Even though you put too much time into the design and washed your hands of it, you still have your pride. You are not about to cut corners with the code. After all, other designers might look at it and judge you!

You work really hard, putting in more work than you probably should have. John even manages to slip in some extra functionality at the scoping phase, which turns out to be a pain in the butt.

For his part, John is wondering what's going on. He hasn't heard from you in weeks. Surely the website must be ready now? He decides to email you to ask how things are progressing. You reply with a short email telling him that everything is progressing smoothly. You never did like project management, and you are sure John would prefer that you spend time building his website instead of writing him detailed reports.

John receives your email and is becoming increasingly frustrated. What does "progressing smoothly" mean? He writes back asking for an expected date of completion, and you reply with a rough estimate.

The date comes and goes without a word from you. After all, it was merely an estimate, and several complications have delayed completion by a few days. John finally loses his temper and calls you. He tells you that he has arranged a marketing campaign to coincide with the launch date, and because he hadn't heard from you, he presumed everything was on schedule.

You defend yourself, citing "scope creep" and unanticipated delays. But responding is difficult when John says, "All I needed was a weekly email keeping me up to date on progress."

EXPLAIN JOHN'S ONGOING ROLE

By this stage, the relationship has broken down entirely. You finish your work, and the website finally launches. Begrudgingly, John pays the invoice after delaying it for as long as possible. What amazes you most is John's pronouncement that he is bitterly disappointed with the result. How can that be when you gave him exactly what he asked for? This guy isn't just thick: he's a jerk!

Of course, John sees things differently. He came to you with a list of his business objectives, and the website has failed to meet any of them. He had hoped to launch the website, watch it achieve his objectives, and then move on to the next project. Instead, after an initial spike in interest, the number of users and inquiries dropped over time, and the website stagnated.

What John does not realize is that websites need continued love and support. You cannot build a website and then abandon it. John has to nurture it by adding new content, engaging with visitors, and planning for ongoing development. If only someone had told him.

THE MORAL OF THE STORY

It's amazing how quick we are to judge our clients. As Web designers, we communicate and empathize for a living. Our job is to communicate messages to our clients' users. We create usable websites by putting ourselves in the position of our users, which allows us to design around their needs.

Why, then, do we so often seem incapable of empathizing or communicating with our clients? Perhaps it is time for us to apply the skills we have cultivated as Web designers to our own customers.

Paul Boag is the founder of UK Web design agency Headscape, author of the Website Owners Manual *and host of award-winning Web design podcast Boagworld.*

107

9

HOW TO IDENTIFY AND DEAL WITH DIFFERENT TYPES OF CLIENTS

By Robert Bowen

IN BUSINESS, BEING able to read people and quickly get a sense of who you're dealing with is an invaluable skill. It turns your encounter with a client into an opportunity to catch a glimpse of the upcoming project and how it will need to be handled. It is one of the building blocks of a professional relationship.

In today's digital age, the arena has shifted to the Web, and the online office space that most freelancers inhabit limits personal interaction. Though sussing out a client's personality via online communication is difficult, it remains an invaluable tool in your arsenal.

In the freelancing field, *you will encounter a range of client types*. Being able to *identify* which type you are dealing with allows you to develop the *right strategy* to maximize your interactions with them, and it could save your sanity. What follows is a list of the most common personality types, the tell-tale signs that will tip you off, and suggestions on how to handle each type.

THE PASSIVE-AGGRESSIVE CLIENT

This is the client who is very passive when you ask for initial input, but when you submit the finished product, they aggressively attack it, demanding a lot of detailed changes, both major and minor. They had an idea of what they wanted all along but kept it mostly to themselves. Even though they showed appreciation of certain ideas and elements throughout the development process, do not expect the passive-aggressive client to keep any of them as they send revisions your way.

IDENTIFYING CHARACTERISTICS

- Communication is mostly one-sided and unhelpful during project development.
- Makes statements such as:
  - "I'm not really sure what we're looking for."
  - "Just do something that would appeal to us generally."
  - "You totally missed the point of what we wanted."

HOW TO DEAL WITH IT

Patience is key. Expecting the last-minute requests for revisions may soften the blow of the client's aggressive behavior. Keep your original layered design intact so that you can easily refine and change it later (not that you wouldn't, but it does happen). Also, make sure your contract specifies a limited number of revisions.

THE FAMILY FRIEND

This is the client whom you have known for years either through personal or family interaction, and this connection has landed you the job. The relationship will be tested and perhaps marred forever by what could very well be a nightmare of a project. This family friend believes he deserves a "special" price and unbridled access to your work. They will sometimes unwittingly belittle your work or not take it seriously because of their personal connection to you.

IDENTIFYING CHARACTERISTICS

- These clients are easy to identify because… well, you know them.
- Makes such statements as:
  - "Could you just throw something together for me?"
  - "I don't want you to think that just because I know you I want you to cut me a deal."
  - "You're going to charge me what?! But we go way back!"

HOW TO DEAL WITH IT

The way to deal with these clients depends on how well you know them and how much you value your relationship with them. But remember that anyone who would take advantage of such a relationship is not truly a friend, so respond accordingly. An honest approach could end up saving the relationship. But start off with a professional, not personal, tone, and they may follow your lead. Of course, if you truly value the relationship, you may want to pass on the job altogether.

THE UNDER-VALUER

Like the family friend, this client devalues your creative contributions. But there is a difference: you do not actually know this person. There is no rationale for their behavior. They feel they should get a "friend's" pricing rate not because they want to be friends with you, but because they do not see your work as being worth that much… even if they couldn't do it themselves. Not coming from a creative background or even having had exposure to the arts can mar someone's appreciation of the work that you do. After years in our field, we make it look easy, and that is what the under-valuer sees.

IDENTIFYING CHARACTERISTICS

- Does not respond to questions in a timely fashion.
- Makes such statements as:
  - "It's not like it takes much effort on your part."
  - "Couldn't you just throw something together for me?"
  - "How hard can this really be?"

HOW TO DEAL WITH IT

Confidence is key here. You know what your work demands and how well you do your job. The under-valuer will recognize this confidence. Don't back down or concede a point to the client when discussing your role in the project. Standing firm will establish the professional and respectful tone you deserve. If the client does not respond in kind, cut your losses and decline their project.

THE NIT-PICKER

This client is never fully satisfied with the work you do and constantly picks on minor details here and there that they dislike and want changed. Do not be surprised if they ask you to change these same details over and over ad nauseam. It is not a sign of disrespect (as it is with the other clients), but simply the nature of the person. They may have been burned in some other project and are now unsatisfied with everything in their path, including your work.

IDENTIFYING CHARACTERISTICS

- Complains almost constantly about unrelated things.
- Personal outlook comes with a scathing bite.
- Makes such statements as:
  - "How hard is it really to [fill in the blank with any rant]?"
  - "I'm not sure about this element here. It just doesn't pop!"
  - "I don't think you're really getting it."

HOW TO DEAL WITH IT

Once again, patience is important (especially if you have some sadistic reason for taking on nit-picking clients). Try to detach yourself from the project as much as possible, so that the constant nit-pickery does not affect you personally. It is easy to feel hurt or get defensive when your work is repeatedly questioned, and you may begin to doubt your skill. But understand that this is not about you or your talent; it is simply a personality trait of the person you are dealing with. And once again, protect yourself in the contract.

THE SCORNFUL SAVER

This client has similarities to the nit-picker and under-valuer but is actually impressed with your work and skill set. They criticize you merely to undermine your confidence in an attempt to lower your pricing rate. Unlike some other client types, the scornful saver understands creative people and their processes. But they are cheap and manipulative, and their scheme may have worked in their favor once or twice in the past. So, they continue to subtly abuse the people they hire in the hope of saving every last penny.

IDENTIFYING CHARACTERISTICS

- Compliments always come with a less-than-flattering qualifier.
- Takes time to respond to questions, sometimes making you ask more than once.
- Makes such statements as:
  - "I really like what you've done overall, but I'm unsure about one or two things."
  - "You may not have gotten exactly what we're looking for, but you're close."

HOW TO DEAL WITH IT

Once again, it is all about confidence. Having a solid understanding of your field and being confident in your knowledge and abilities will keep this client's manipulation in check. Standing your ground and even calling the client on some of their tactics could shift the balance of power over to you. Be prepared to walk away from the project if the disrespect and manipulation continues. There will be other projects and other clients.

THE "I-COULD-DO-THIS-MYSELF"-ER

Where to begin… When this client farms a project out to you, they make clear to you that they know how to do what they're hiring you to do but they just don't have the time to actually do it. They may be working at a firm or as an entrepreneur; either way, you are there to pick up their slack. If they're at a firm, you could be in for an interesting situation; they were likely hired for their particular style and proposals, and now you will have to please two sets of people: the person who hired you and the people who hired him.

IDENTIFYING CHARACTERISTICS

- Will generally be (or look) hectic and rushed.
- Communication from them often takes the form of short bursts of information.
- Makes such statements as:
  - "I could easily handle this if my schedule weren't so full."
  - "Really? Not sure that's the direction I would've gone in, but whatever."
  - "Remember, you are filling my shoes, and they're pretty big."

HOW TO DEAL WITH IT

The "I-Could-Do-This-Myself"-er will likely have recognized your talent and skill right away, which is why they hired you. They merely want you to know that this project (and thus you) is not above their ability. And though these reminders will grate on you periodically, they will let you run with your ideas, perhaps offering suggestions or feedback on the final design.

THE CONTROL FREAK

This client desperately needs to micro-manage every little detail of the project, no matter their qualifications. No decision may be made without their explicit input and approval. This tiresome person forces himself into your workflow, heedless of either invitation or protest, and demands access to you at whim. The concepts of boundaries and strict work processes are easily lost on the control freak, who constantly disrupts the flow. They may also believe you lack dedication or preparedness, further reinforcing their need to interfere.

IDENTIFYING CHARACTERISTICS

- Initial contact is long, detailed, and one-sided, with little input sought from you.
- Your input remains unsought as the project pushes forward.
- Makes such statements as:
  - "This way we can keep in contact 24/7 in case you have any questions, or I do."
  - "I really know best what is right for the project and what is not."
  - "What do you mean, I'm distracting you? I am the only thing keeping this project on track!"

HOW TO DEAL WITH IT

If you absolutely must take on this client, for whatever reason, resign yourself to the fact that you will not be steering at any point. You will have to detach yourself from the work because you will have no control at all. You will merely be constructing, not designing, so just let go and let it happen. You may want to exclude this project from your portfolio.

THE DREAM CLIENT

This client, widely dismissed as a myth, does in fact exist and understands the full scope and artistry of your work. They value your role and creative contributions and want you in the driver's seat as soon as the project gets underway. They are timely with responses and payments... payments that they did not "negotiate" but rather accepted for what they are. They reflect on your suggestions and have confidence in your capabilities.

IDENTIFYING CHARACTERISTICS

- Is enthusiastic about the project and your involvement in it.
- Communication shows awareness of and respect for your role.
- Makes such statements as:
  - "Here's the brief we prepared. The rest is pretty much up to you."
  - "We like what we've seen and trust you'll do great things for us."

HOW TO DEAL WITH IT

Don't brag! Just enjoy the ride and hold on to them for as long as you possibly can!

WRAP-UP

Being able to identify the type of client you are dealing with will prepare you for the job ahead. It will also help you decide whether to accept the job in the first place. Your contract will reflect the power dynamics of the project, so the more you know about the client, the better able you will be to adjust the contract as necessary.

Robert Bowen is an emerging author, celebrated podcaster, and poet, and most recently the co-founder and imaginative co-contributor of the creative design and blogging duo at the Arbenting Freebies Blog *and Dead Wings Designs.*

10

HOW TO RESPOND EFFECTIVELY TO DESIGN CRITICISM

By Andrew Follett

WINSTON CHURCHILL ONCE said: "Criticism may not be agreeable, but it is necessary. It fulfills the same function as pain in the human body. It calls attention to an unhealthy state of things." Regardless of where you work or who you work for, being able to take criticism is part of the job. Whether you're getting feedback from your boss or a client, having a proper perspective on criticism and a sound understanding of how to use it effectively is important.

Unfortunately, not many people enjoy criticism. In fact, many have developed a thick skin and take pride in their ability to brush it off and move on. However, despite its negative connotation, *criticism often presents excellent opportunities to grow* as a designer. Before you can respond effectively, you need to understand what those opportunities are.

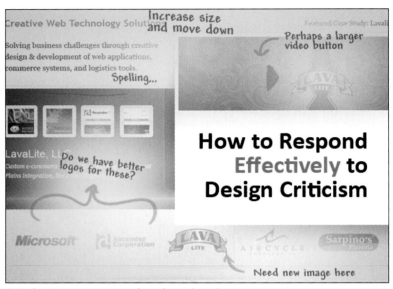

Think of criticism as an opportunity for professional growth.

Let's look at some important aspects of getting constructive criticism:

- *Uncover blind spots:* Doing your own thing is easy, but your habits will eventually become deeply ingrained and hard to break. Criticism gives you a vital outside perspective on your work, uncovering potential areas for improvement that you are unable to see by yourself.

- *Challenge yourself:* Feedback challenges you to be a better designer. Rather than settle for your own standards, you are pushed to take your work to the next level.

- *Develop communication skills:* If nothing else, dealing with a critic can dramatically improve the way you communicate — an essential skill for any successful design career.

- *Outside motivation:* Constructive criticism often gives you the kick in the butt you need to learn a new design skill or technique. Self-motivation is great, but everyone could use a hand from time to time.

- *A lesson in humility:* Never underestimate the importance of humility. Although criticism can bruise the ego, it keeps you grounded, making you easier to work with and more open to learning from others.

A positive view of criticism isn't enough. You also need to know how to respond effectively when it comes. Here are eight tips you can use to start making the most of criticism today.

HAVE THE RIGHT ATTITUDE

Design is subjective and, like any art form, has no rulebook. No one can tell you what is "right" and "wrong" with your work, but that doesn't mean you can completely ignore your boss's or client's opinion either. However, by taking criticism and feedback with the right attitude, you can use it to your advantage and even enjoy it.

Everyone looks at design through a filter shaped by personal experience, and others' filters are usually very different from your own. While you may have a degree in design and 10 years of experience, not everyone will agree with your "expert" opinion, so don't expect them to. The important thing is to have a proper attitude from the beginning. Expect others to disagree with you, and be open to new perspectives. Align your expectations and understand that criticism is part of the process. While harsh criticism can cut deep and even scar, it can also motivate, instruct, and do all of the good things mentioned earlier.

Last, but not least, try to remove yourself from the criticism and view it as a commentary on your actions or work and not as a personal attack. While easier said than done, this distinction is key to responding effectively. If you can rise above the criticism and respond calmly and effectively, you will not only earn the admiration of your critic but feel better doing it. Set the right expectations, understand the benefits, remove yourself from the equation, and remember — attitude truly is everything.

CLARIFY THE OBJECTIVE

Clearly identifying the goal of a design before you share it with others is always a good idea. Are you showing it off to mom for some fridge time? Is it a client who's trying to solve a business challenge through design? Or perhaps you're consulting a friend with no experience or stake in the project.

Regardless, a vague or confused objective will always elicit off-target feedback, so make sure everyone involved "gets it" before taking action.

To respond effectively to criticism, you need to be sure that the critic understands your goals. Be specific. Present your objective in clear and concise terms; the criticism you receive will be targeted and actionable as a result.

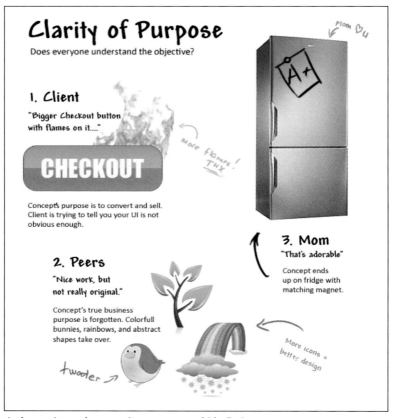

Clarify your objective for your audience to ensure useful feedback.

CHECK YOUR FIRST REACTION

For most people (me included), the first reaction to criticism is to get defensive or even lash out. If this sounds like you, take time to develop the habit of taking a deep breath and counting to 10 before responding. This simple yet effective method gives you a chance to regain composure and allow logic to prevail over emotion. The last thing you want to do is get overly emotional and give a response that you will later regret. Remember, in most cases, your critic is only trying to help you.

Despite the initial sting, you need honest feedback to become a better designer. This is especially important for enthusiasts or beginners in the trade. All visual arts have an intrinsic reward mechanism: the more you create, the more you sense the progression of your skill.

It's a loop that keeps all artists going, and when this euphoric moment is crushed by accurate and much-needed criticism, recovering may be difficult. Keep in mind, though, that your skill and perceptiveness in this field will mature over time. If you have the right attitude to begin with, the proper response will follow.

SEPARATE THE WHEAT FROM THE CHAFF

Unfortunately, not all criticism is constructive. Some people are in a bad mood, bitter, or just plain negative and will take any chance to put others down. Some are also inexperienced or unqualified to give you valuable feedback. While design is subjective, being able to separate useful feedback from cheap shots and misinformation is important. However, this is not an excuse to ignore comments that you don't like. Unless you believe a critique was given in malice or ignorance, don't be quick to dismiss it.

Here are a few tips to distinguish between the two:

- *Specific:* Valuable feedback is always specific. It is clear, logical and defined. "The logo is ugly" or "I don't like the color choice" are examples of useless criticism (if you get a lot of this, see the "Dig Deeper When Necessary" section later in this chapter).
- *Actionable:* Constructive criticism should enable you to take immediate action. You should come away with a clearer idea of how to improve the concept and the path to follow.
- *Objective:* Useful feedback is unbiased. It gives you a unique perspective without an ulterior motive. Objective criticism will always be even-tempered and appropriate.

LEARN FROM IT

This step is possibly the hardest one in this learning experience but by far the most important. For criticism to serve its purpose, you need to act on it! Don't just go back to business as usual; make an effort to improve. The great thing about criticism is that it uncovers our blind spots, weaknesses that only others can see. When you're confronted by criticism, don't let the opportunity pass: write it down and do whatever it takes to change for the better.

If someone criticizes your copywriting skills, start with baby steps. Read a relevant blog once a week. Buy a book. Practice writing headlines for 10 minutes each day. Small victories are often the quickest path to success. Eventually you will improve and have your critic to thank.

LOOK FOR A NEW IDEA

If you can't learn anything new, look for a new idea. A different perspective gives you a chance to examine your work from a viewpoint that you would never have considered otherwise. Just as you get inspiration from a gallery or another talented designer, you can find ideas and inspiration in constructive criticism; seeing it just requires you to step back. Be curious, and approach the criticism objectively; it could be incredibly useful.

Criticism is sometimes the cold shower you need to wake up and hit the "Reset" button on a project. Remember, your work is based on your own preconceived notions of what the client wants, and you should always be open to the possibility that you have missed the mark. In the event that you do need to start over, discuss the objectives and expectations right away. Clarifying this information in the first place might have prevented a re-do altogether.

DIG DEEPER WHEN NECESSARY

At some point, everyone has received vague, unclear, or unactionable feedback. It's a part of life. Unfortunately, unless you take the initiative, this type of feedback is useless to everyone involved. However, if you're willing to dig a little deeper, you may uncover things that no one else was willing to tell you. Start by asking open-ended questions that get to the core of the issue, questions like, "I want to understand your point of view. Could you please provide more detail?" or "How can I improve?" Ask for specifics and, above all else, honesty. These kinds of questions will help keep communication lines open and allow you to walk away with practical and concrete advice.

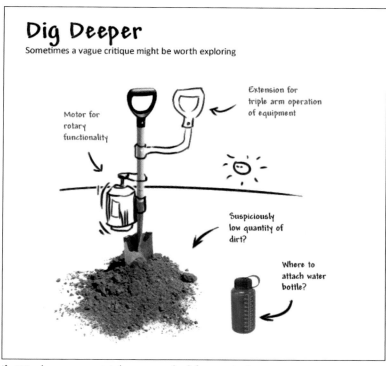

Dig Deeper

Sometimes a vague critique might be worth exploring

Motor for
rotary
functionality

Extension for
triple arm operation
of equipment

Suspiciously
low quantity of
dirt?

Where to
attach water
bottle?

123

If criticism leaves you uncertain how to proceed, ask for more details.

If you feel uncomfortable asking your critic for more detail, or if they are unwilling to provide it, approach someone you respect and trust and ask them what they think. Do they agree with the criticism? Why or why not? Assuming this person is honest and knowledgeable, you should be able to get the answers that you need to move forward.

THANK THE CRITIC

Whether the criticism you receive is genuine or downright rude, make a point of saying "Thank you." Thanking even your harshest critics can create a lasting impression, keep you humble, and open the door to additional feedback in the future. Expressing gratitude will also make you feel better about the experience and help you alleviate any innate avoidance of feedback and criticism you may have. If you have followed these guidelines and recognize the true value of the criticism you have received, saying "Thank you" shouldn't be too difficult.

If you respect the person and their opinion, go one step further and develop a long-term mentoring relationship with them. Much like in the old days of craftsman and apprentice, a relationship with an individual whose opinion you value can go a long way in developing your skills and abilities. If nothing else, a mentor can keep you accountable to your work and help you continually improve.

Andrew Follett is a small-business marketing director and founder of Concept Feedback (`www.conceptfeedback.com/`*), a community of designers and marketers dedicated to sharing ideas and feedback on design projects.*

11

CHAPTER 11

WEB DESIGNER'S GUIDE TO PROFESSIONAL NETWORKING

By Steven Snell

PROFESSIONAL NETWORKING IS a critical component to a successful career as a designer. Whether it be for finding new clients or identifying opportunities for growth and improvement, a strong network of contacts is extremely valuable. In this chapter, we take a detailed look at the potential benefits of networking, and offer tips that can be used in your own networking efforts.

Networking involves building connections and relationships with people from various backgrounds and professions, including other designers and developers. This chapter was written with Web designers in mind, but the principles are generally applicable to any profession — although the specifics may vary.

WHY NETWORK?

If you haven't been actively involved in networking, you may be wondering why you should even bother with it. Before we get into the tips and suggestions for networking, let's take a look at some of the benefits.

REFERRALS

Word-of-mouth advertising is a leading source of business for many designers. Simply put, if more people know about you and your services, you'll have more opportunities for referrals. By getting connected and staying in touch with those in your network you will be on their mind when someone they know is in need of the services that you provide. A potential client who gets a personal recommendation from someone who knows you or has worked with you will be much more likely to become a paying client than someone with another type of lead.

Much of the networking done by designers is with others who offer the same or very similar services. Obtaining referral business through a network of designers is more common than you might think. Although your services may have some overlap with another designer in your network, you're each going to have some unique strengths and weaknesses, as well as varying levels of experience with different types of clients. Additionally, there could be some types of work that others simply don't like to take, or situations where schedules and deadlines make it impossible for a designer to work with a particular client. In situations like these, it's very common for the designer to recommend a friend or colleague.

COLLABORATION

Especially for freelancers and independent designers, having a strong network opens up countless possibilities for collaborating. This could be a one-time thing that arises from the needs of a particular project, or it could be an ongoing collaboration. Ideally, your network will include a number of people who have skills that complement yours. This will allow you to work with others and each focus on what you do best.

PROBLEM-SOLVING

If you trust and value the people in your network, you will not hesitate to turn to them when you need some advice or help with a problem. Do you know someone who has been through a similar situation and could give you some advice from their own experience? For designers and developers, this could be a technical issue, such as dealing with a coding challenge or determining the best solution to a client's needs, or it could simply be a need for guidance in some aspect of running a freelance business. There are many projects that help designers and developers solve design or programming issues, such as the Stack Overflow (`stackoverflow.com`), a platform for designers and developers to share their experiences, ideas, and thoughts.

Stack Overflow is a collaboratively edited question-and-answer website where programmers can solve problems and network.

© 2010 stack overflow internet services, inc

FUTURE OPPORTUNITIES

A professional who is well-connected will typically have more opportunities than a comparably skilled professional who is not well-connected. You may have no pressing reason today for a strong network of contacts, but you could run into a situation in the future when having others you can count on would be invaluable.

For freelance designers, maybe you don't want to freelance forever, and when you're ready to start looking for employment the process will be much easier if you already have an established network that knows you and the quality of your work. Yes, you could wait to do your networking when you've officially stopped freelancing, but you'll be better off if you have established some relationships before then.

HELP OTHERS

So far, everything we've discussed has focused on what your network can do for you, but true networking is not one-sided. One of the benefits of being well connected is that you will have plenty of opportunities to help others. Perhaps you won't be the freelancer who is looking for employment, but maybe you will be the contact who puts a freelancing friend in contact with someone who's looking to hire a designer.

FRIENDSHIPS

Aside from all of the professional benefits, networking can be a fun way to meet new people and build friendships. This can be especially valuable for freelancers and others who work from home. Networking may be one of the few opportunities you have to interact with other professionals in your field.

NETWORKING TIPS FOR DESIGNERS

Now that we have looked at some benefits of networking, here are some tips you can put into practice.

BE ACCESSIBLE

One of the keys to being well connected is making it possible for others to reach you. Sure, networking is about your efforts to meet others, but it also involves being accessible when people want to get in touch with you. This could include having a contact form or email address on your portfolio website, being involved at social networks, linking to your social profiles from your portfolio, and responding to people when they reach out to you.

SEEK MUTUAL BENEFIT

The most successful types of networking relationships are the "win-win" ones — those in which both parties benefit in one way or another. If you want networking to have a major impact on your business or career, make the effort to find opportunities for mutual benefit. These situations will encourage both parties to keep the relationship strong and improve it in any way possible, bringing results that could not be accomplished individually.

Finding win-win situations is not easy, but they will present themselves when you get to know others very well and you all can see each other's unique strengths, abilities and opportunities. These types of networks will more likely lead to stronger, long-lasting relationships.

BLOG

Many designers maintain a blog on their portfolio website or other domain. Blogging is not only effective in attracting potential clients but is also a great way to get involved with other designers and build a network. Blogging is personal in nature and involves two-way communication, making it extremely conducive to interaction. Bloggers tend to read other blogs as well, and the design blogging community is very active. Blogging is a great way to get exposure and open up opportunities to meet other professionals.

FOCUS ON DEPTH OF RELATIONSHIPS

Like just about anything else in life, quality is better than quantity. While having connections with a wide variety of people is good, you'll find that your most significant benefits from networking come from your closest relationships. As you connect with people, get to know them on more than a superficial level. The people with whom you build strong relationships will likely become part of the "inner circle" that you reach out to on a consistent basis.

BE PROACTIVE

Don't sit back and wait for others to approach you. Get involved in social networks, go to local networking events, attend seminars, and approach people who you'd like to get to know. If you're at an event or using an online social network, the other people are there for the same reasons as you — so don't be intimidated by the thought of approaching them.

This could also include commenting on design blogs, participating in forums, and writing guest articles. Your network will be a valuable part of your career, so be proactive and work to make it something special.

KNOW WHAT YOU'RE LOOKING FOR

If you're proactively getting to know other professionals, it helps to know what you're looking for in potential contacts. This allows you to identify the right people to approach, making your networking efforts more effective and efficient. For example, if you're a student who will be graduating in a year and looking for a job as a designer, it would be beneficial to connect with people who run design studios or people who work at places that may be hiring designers. If you're a designer who doesn't do any development work, it would be beneficial to know some good developers who you could team up with on projects.

Think of your strengths, weaknesses, and situation. Who or what would help you get to where you want to be? Identify people who are in these ideal positions and get to know them.

KNOW WHAT YOU HAVE TO OFFER

Just as important as knowing what you're looking for in others, you should also be aware of what you can offer others and why you would be a valuable member of their network. Think about what is unique and special about your skills and the opportunities you could present to others.

Of course, this doesn't mean you should go around telling everyone exactly what you can offer them and why they need you, but having a clear sense of your own worth helps you identify ideal situations of mutual benefit and how to present yourself in ways that make you stand out.

NETWORK INDIRECTLY

Some of your best contacts will not be people who you actually need to keep in touch with. Rather, you may have a contact who knows the type of person you're looking for and can act as a gateway or messenger to them. Your network becomes exponentially more powerful and valuable when you realize that you're connected not only to the people who you know directly, but also to all of the people who they know, too.

The social networking website LinkedIn offers a good way to visualize this concept. You may be connected to 50 people on LinkedIn, but each of those people will be connected to others who you don't know. If each of your contacts is connected to another 50 people, you're only one person away from some potentially valuable relationships.

Practically speaking, if you're looking for someone with a particular skill or experience, talk to others in your network to see who they know who may fit the description. Indirect networking is often more effective than direct, because it leverages the networks of others and gives you opportunities to get recommendations from people you trust.

DON'T WAIT UNTIL YOU NEED SOMETHING

Networking is more effective when it's not done under the pressure of needing to produce immediate results. Reaching out to your friends and contacts when you need something is natural, but having a large and established network that stands ready to help when the need arises is more effective. Networking only when you need something is unlikely to result in mutual benefit and could give others the impression that you're interested only in helping yourself.

HELP WHENEVER POSSIBLE

Helping others and making yourself a valuable contact and friend to others is a big part of networking. You will not always be in a position to help, but avoid the temptation of helping others only when there's something in it for you. A network of people who are willing and eager to help each other will be positive for everyone.

DON'T "USE" PEOPLE

When looking for the right people to build your network, thinking only of what other people can do for you is all too easy. But that's not an effective way to interact, and they will often see through your efforts.

The best way to avoid using people is by looking for situations in which you can help them. By emphasizing your value to them rather than how they can help you, you'll avoid seeing them only for what they have to offer. If you focus on helping others, they will likely want to find ways to help you in return.

DON'T LET NETWORKING HURT YOUR PRODUCTIVITY

Although professional networking should be an integral part of your work, it's not going to put money in your pocket directly. Freelancers in particular need to stay focused on providing services to clients in order to generate the income that keeps them going. Networking is important, but it should not interfere with your core operations.

Online networks and email especially can be distractions. Develop a system that allows you to interact with others in a way that doesn't hinder your work. For example, rather than leaving your email and Twitter account open all day, set specific times to check them. Each person is different and has a way that works best for them, so find one that allows you to network with maximum benefit and with minimum disturbance to your productivity.

DON'T EVALUATE PEOPLE TOO QUICKLY

When you're focused on strengthening your network by making valuable connections, it's easy to start measuring people by what they can bring to the table. This is a dangerous habit because it will make you reluctant to get to know some people because you don't think they have much to offer. They may have hidden talents that take a little time or effort to discover.

DON'T TRY TO BE EVERYWHERE ONLINE

Plenty of opportunities are available to network, particularly online. But you can be active in only so many places, so don't spread yourself too thin. Instead, choose a few networking websites and groups that show promise, and you'll find that you have more time to be active.

Being active in a few circles yields better results than having limited activity in many circles. This goes back to the need for quality over quantity in building relationships.

ATTEND EVENTS

Web designers and other online professionals are fortunate to have a number of high-quality conferences and events in their industry that provide opportunities to learn and network. If an event is taking place in your area, check it out. Of course, if you're willing to travel, you could attend events anywhere.

PAY ATTENTION TO LOCAL OPPORTUNITIES

One of the traps of online networking is that it can cause you to miss opportunities for face-to-face networking in your local area. Many localities have chamber of commerce events, business card exchanges, seminars, and other events at which to connect with local professionals. Pay attention to these activities in your area in case they offer something that warrants your involvement.

Steven Snell has been designing websites for several years. He actively maintains a few blogs of his own, including DesignM.ag, which regularly provides articles and resources for web designers.

GROUP INTERVIEW: EXPERT ADVICE FOR STUDENTS AND YOUNG WEB DESIGNERS

By Steven Snell

OUR READERS HAVE requested that Smashing Magazine conduct *an interview with industry leaders on issues that are relevant to students and those just starting off in their design careers.* With the help of our panel of 16 designers, we'll dispense advice that should help new designers get their careers off to a promising start. We've asked a few different questions of each of the designers; you'll see all of their responses in this chapter.

Here is a list of the designers who participated:

- Henry Jones (Web Design Ledger)
- Wolfgang Bartelme (Bartelme.at)
- Chris Coyier (CSS-Tricks)
- Chris Spooner (SpoonGraphics, Line25)
- Soh Tanaka
- Jon Philips (Spyre Studios)
- Paul Boag (Boagworld, Headscape)
- David Leggett (Tutorial9, UX Booth)
- Jacob Gube (Six Revisions)
- Elliot Jay Stocks

- Brian Hoff (The Design Cubicle)
- Darren Hoyt
- Walter Apai (Webdesigner Depot)
- Jacob Cass (Just Creative Design)
- Zach Dunn (One Mighty Roar and Build Internet)
- Paul Andrew (Speckyboy Design Magazine)

For students who aspire to work in design, what would you recommend they study?

David Leggett: Finding a good university-level design program that interests you will greatly increase your chance of finding awesome opportunities down the road, but it's very beneficial to get experience before and outside of your education. Find projects to help with, start your own, read up and apply as much as you can while you're learning on the side. The extra experience never hurts, and at the very least you'll get to see if design is something you really enjoy.

Just to clarify, I have never taken any higher education courses in design, but I know that the knowledge you get in that environment is valuable, as I'm sure others will suggest.

Wolfgang Bartelme: Well, I guess the most important thing is "practice, practice, practice." To improve the quality of your work, you have to keep pushing yourself further and further. By the way, many great artists are self-taught. But I'm also convinced that a profound education will sharpen your skills and help you be able to judge why and how certain designs work. Personally, I studied information design at the University of Applied Science in Graz, focusing on all different aspects of design: print and advertising, exhibitions, Web design, usability, photography, and film — which would give students a broad knowledge base and make them more generalists than specialists.

How does a student determine whether design is for them or they should pursue another career?

Jacob Gube: This is a question you have to ask yourself. There aren't any set rules or algorithms to determine whether you should be a designer. The important thing is to have passion for the work. Even mediocre designers will be able to sustain themselves, but they'll have to work extra hard to compete with more talented and experienced designers. So, it all boils down to how much you want to be a designer and how much you're willing to work at it and push forward. I won't sugar-coat the current situation: the truth is that the industry is saturated, and there are a lot more designers than jobs, so you have to be sure that this is the profession you want to invest your time in.

Henry Jones: I think it's all about passion. If you find yourself up late at night working on design projects just for the fun of it, then that's a good sign that design is right for you. I think one of the worst situations in life is hating what you do. Loving what you do means you'll probably be doing it and thinking about it even outside of class or when you're not being paid to do it. You'll constantly be honing your skills and staying on top of the latest technologies, which is very important for designers.

David Leggett: Everyone has a unique situation, and I don't mean to suggest the following is always true: if you're already a student at a university and have no outside experience, it may be difficult to really pursue a career in design. I say this only because personal friends of mine have struggled to find jobs in this current economic climate. Having experience and something to show for your knowledge goes a long way.

Otherwise, be sure that you truly enjoy whatever you decide to pursue. Many designers and artists I've met thoroughly enjoy their lifestyles, even when they're struggling to find work. This is not to say that you should undervalue your work, but if you enjoy your career when you're not making money, then it's probably a good match for you.

Wolfgang Bartelme: First and foremost, designing stuff has to be fun: you have to love what you do. If that's not the case, look for something else. Secondly, you should, of course, have a decent measure of talent and imagination. Even though you will learn many skills in the course of your studies, without talent and imagination, your work will be at best mediocre.

Chris Spooner: As with any career, if you're passionate about the subject, you're set to succeed. Careers in the design industry can seem exciting; after all, all you do is sit and color things in all day, right? I think this draws in a lot of people who maybe haven't been particularly creative in the past and see the career as easy.

This type of person might then find it difficult to be motivated to learn the required skills and to continue developing those skills throughout their career. That's not to say that if you weren't a creative child, you can't pursue a career in design. We all stumble across different interests throughout our lives, so as long as you feel you have a passion for design, go for it!

How do you balance education and work?

Zach Dunn: By my last estimate, I spend about three to four hours on client work for every one hour of academic work. I generally learn specialized skills more from client work than from academics. It's easy to get caught up in client work and blogging. The hard part is making sure you don't lose touch with the world around you. Interacting with clients and blog community members is certainly social, but you need to take a break and interact with "regular college students" from time to time. I consider it like mental detox.

I'm convinced you must put in extra time on personal projects to truly become competent in the Web design industry. Going through the motions during class and homework hours only leaves you behind. The Internet moves faster than any standard academic schedule. Keeping current and practiced is up to you.

Jacob Cass: Finding the right balance between family, friends, work, and all of life's other misdemeanors will always be a challenge, no matter what your career. You must set priorities and goals relative to what you want to achieve and get out of life. Although I have now finished studying (formally), I could say that my biggest challenge then was finding enough time to give high-quality attention to all projects, whether they were educational, personal, or for paying customers. At times, I found this nearly impossible, and to be honest a lot of my university and personal work suffered from my commitments to paying customers. In saying this, I guess a lot of it comes down to having priorities, goals, and good time management.

How did work outside of your studies prepare you for your career?

Zach Dunn: Almost all of our "career" success so far has been a direct result of work done outside of studies. College is a great incubator for a number of things other than academics. I value school for reasons that are different than those of the average person. College has helped me socially. Sam [Dunn] recently wrote an article on BuildInternet.com that does a great job of explaining more about our college philosophy in relation to Web design, titled "The Role of College for Web Designers."

Certain careers cannot start before graduation. Lawyers, for example, can't have hobby clients while putting themselves through school: it's all or nothing. Web design isn't limited by credentials for entry. Web design is largely portfolio-based. When's the last time a client was more interested in your GPA than in your previous client work? In this industry, we have the luxury of starting early. I like to take advantage of that.

I don't know what the future holds for Sam and me, but I'm confident that at least some of the projects we start today will have some role in it.

Jacob Cass: To be honest, I learned more in six months of blogging and following other people's blogs, than studying for three full years at university. Doing extra work outside of the education system is vital.

What should students and new designers focus on outside of their course work to advance in their careers?

Brian Hoff: Students should definitely consider taking many business classes, especially if they want to go freelance or start their own studio one day. I've always been passionate enough about design to teach myself, but I wish I had taken more business and marketing classes. Also, I would recommend collecting designs. Having resources for inspiration and an idea of good design is essential. I take photos of many types, colors, designs, etc. as I pass them by, and I use LittleSnapper to organize online media. Being a graphic designer is non-stop learning.

Chris Coyier: No individual program is going to cover every single angle of design, especially the most modern technological stuff. Because you are already reading Smashing Magazine, you probably already have a good grasp of what's going on in modern design. Reading and following tutorials and doing your own experimental projects on the side will definitely help you excel. That being said, your whole life doesn't have to revolve around career enhancement. A well-rounded life will serve you well. Perhaps some of your other hobbies could benefit from your design talent. I have a friend who used to build coffee tables and decorate the surfaces with patterns of partially burnt matches. If he were looking for a design job, I would absolutely tell him to put that stuff onto an online portfolio.

Elliot Jay Stocks: Build your portfolio. Do free websites for your mates' bands or your Mum's friend's wool shop. It might not be glamorous work, but doing as much as you can builds up your portfolio, and you'll learn loads on every project. When I left university and got my first job, my portfolio was made up almost entirely of stuff I'd done on an extracurricular basis, not really the coursework itself. But also don't forget that it's about quality, not quantity, and a good portfolio strikes a balance between variety (showing that you're versatile) and continuity (showing that you have your own identity as a designer).

Walter Apai: It's important to expand your knowledge to any areas that are related to design. Most design courses concentrate on the basics or on how to use the various pieces of software that are available. These are just basic tools for new designers, but they won't make you a great designer.

Learn about art, layout, and composition, and try to read at least one new book on design every month, or even one per week. Subscribe to design blogs such as Smashing Magazine and Webdesigner Depot, and never stop learning. Keep updating your knowledge whenever possible by attending conferences, reading books and magazines, and becoming involved in the local artistic community. Try to become a well-rounded designer, not just an operator of Photoshop or another design software tool.

George Lois, the real-life inspiration for Don Draper in *Mad Men,* said it best:

> *The computer has played a role in destroying creativity with Photoshop. Everybody thinks they're a designer.*

While he may be generalizing a bit, I believe what is meant is that you can't be a proper designer without understanding the fundamentals of art and design.

Jacob Gube: When I was a college student, what truly helped me in my career was proactively attempting to get real-world experience by doing freelance work, part time. The purpose was two-fold: to see what it was like to work with the kind of people who would become your employers once you were out of school, and to apply what you learned in class, which reinforces your education and helps you understand it hands on. You might even end up with a few portfolio pieces to show employers once you're on the job hunt — and some money to buy those expensive classroom textbooks.

What one thing do you wish you knew before starting your career?

Darren Hoyt: Being in touch with my limitations and skills. The first few years of designing for the Web (1998 to 2001), I knew that being cross-trained was important, so I built my skills in design and front-end code (HTML, CSS) equally. But then I made the mistake of thinking that, if I was to become a more complete designer and developer, I should learn Perl, Flash, and Unix commands, too. I sucked at all of those things and kept sucking until they asked me to stop.

Deep down, I knew I wasn't wired for any of that stuff. And more importantly, I wasn't actually interested in it, not compared to design anyway. Employers do value someone who is cross-trained, but not if the results are mediocre.

David Leggett: Pleasing everyone is nearly impossible. Be friendly to those who enjoy your work and friendlier to those who attack it.

Jacob Gube: I wished I had realized that quality is more important than quantity. When I started out, I focused on low-cost, high-quantity jobs, which resulted in late hours, not enough pay and nothing really that I could be proud to put in my portfolio. I wanted to work with as many people and on as many projects as I could to jumpstart my experience and resume. But the Project Triangle principle applies here: I did it fast and cheap, and so the outcomes weren't good. If I had slowed down and focused on getting gigs that were interesting and better quality, I would have progressed more fruitfully.

Paul Boag: That constraints are good. As a Web design student, I was given endless freedom to design how I wanted and what I wanted. However, the real world is not like that. When I joined IBM out of university, my first job was to design 8-bit icons. Very restrictive indeed. When I started on the Web, it allowed only gray backgrounds and text that was justified left, right, or centered. The first time I worked on a multimedia CD, it was capable of running video at only 160 x 120 pixels.

At the time, this frustrated me massively. However, in hindsight it was enormously beneficial. It pushed me creatively, and it has also given me a lot more patience with the peculiarities of browsers such as IE6.

What job search advice do you have for recent graduates?

Soh Tanaka: First and foremost, get your portfolio up, and make sure it represents your best work. If you lack work samples, start creating projects for yourself (websites for your hobbies, your family or for friends). As a new grad, you need to prove that you are serious and willing; the best way to get that message across is through a robust portfolio.

Secondly, hit the job boards, and send your resumes and cover letters to companies you would like to work for. Doing research and tailoring each cover letter and resume to the company is important. Stick to the job requirements, and follow directions carefully. These employers receive many applications daily, and nothing is worse than seeing a bland and generic introduction to who you are and what you offer. Stand out from the rest.

Thirdly, keep your networks open, and make yourself known! Networking is key.

Darren Hoyt: Obviously, scour the online job boards, but also follow the blogs and Twitter feeds of Web designers whom you respect. Studying their methods will give you a clearer picture of the sort of designer you want to be. If you need advice, trying dropping them an email. But remember that not everyone has the time to answer.

Truthfully, most designers I know didn't get their job by applying cold to an agency they knew nothing about. Instead, they slowly made relationships with like-minded people until they began to see opportunities and get offers.

But I would stress, don't "network" compulsively. It can look obvious and obnoxious and make you look needy. Instead, make connections with people you think you actually share interests with, people you can picture as colleagues and friends rather than business contacts. The rewards are much greater.

Chris Coyier: Nobody will hire you because you say you have skills. You'll have to demonstrate your skills, so either work on your current personal website or start building one. Use the website as a portfolio and resume to send to companies. Send it both to companies that say they are hiring and to ones that don't. Just because a Web company doesn't hang a "Now hiring" sign on its door doesn't mean it couldn't use someone. Pitch them. A little advice for that portfolio: three awesome designs are better than three awesome and six mediocre designs packed in the same space. Showcase only your finest work. Quality over quantity.

What should new designers consider when deciding between working for an agency and freelancing?

Elliot Jay Stocks: Jumping straight into freelancing once you've completed your education is really tempting. I very nearly did that myself. But I'm glad I didn't. You learn valuable lessons working for someone else first, and it's actually much easier because you don't have to worry about getting clients for yourself. So, I would recommend working for someone else before going it alone. It's a great opportunity to build your portfolio without dealing with any of the boring stuff that goes with freelancing or running your own business.

Soh Tanaka: As a new designer, being at an agency or on a team is great for learning and feeling out the industry. Though you may not be able to set your own hours or work from home, a steady pay check and health insurance are both welcome during a tough economy.

When choosing the freelance route, have some experience under your belt, and be ready to be on your own. The key factor is knowing what your skills are and having discipline. Freelancing has its ups and downs, and you must be self-motivated and determined to overcome the challenges. Working from home and setting your own hours is ideal for most, but young designers should consider the requirements and reality before diving in head first. It may be wise to freelance only part time until you build enough confidence and experience and know enough about your strengths and weaknesses to be able to make the right decisions when you strike out on your own.

Chris Spooner: It's always worth learning the pros and cons of working for an agency and freelancing, because each has its perks! Here are a few that spring to mind.

- **Agency pros:**
  - Working for an agency after your studies can be great for gaining experience in how the industry works and how projects are managed from start to finish.
  - At an agency, you work with like-minded colleagues, whom you can learn from and develop with.
  - Large agencies often attract big corporations and established brands.
  - A full-time job guarantees you a monthly wage and set working hours.

141

- **Agency cons:**
  - You might get stuck working on projects that you don't find interesting or might have to work on something you don't agree with.
  - Agencies sometimes have strict policies, rules, and guidelines. For instance, browsing the Web, checking Facebook, or tweeting might get you a slap on the wrist.
  - Agencies work during the usual 9:00 to 5:00 business hours, so you will have to as well.
- **Freelance pros:**
  - As a freelancer, you have complete control of the projects you take on and the type of work you do.
  - You're not tied to any particular working hours, so taking a day off is no problem.
  - If you can generate a consistent flow of projects, earning a decent wage can be much easier than it would be working at an agency.
  - You can work in your pajamas!
- **Freelance cons:**
  - You are personally responsible for your own income, a circumstance that can put you at risk.
  - Freelancers need to be able to manage their time in order to avoid distractions.

I would recommend that new designers first seek out employment, which will give them professional experience with and knowledge of design. Then they'll be able to decide whether they fit better at an agency or working for themselves.

One of the main things to consider before starting out as a freelancer is whether you've generated enough industry experience to be able not only to create designs but to source work, manage multiple projects, and communicate with clients. These other factors definitely come into play when freelancing, so having at least some knowledge of these processes before diving in is important.

How can students and young designers make themselves more valuable to potential employers?

Darren Hoyt: Start building a Web presence as early as possible, even before seeking a junior position. Buy a personal domain and set up a simple portfolio, with an "About" page that gives a snapshot of your personality and talents. If you haven't done client work, do pro bono projects for friends until you have work samples to show. Displaying them publicly shows that you have pride in your work.

Be concise. Employers and human resource people are like anyone else: they are busy and have short attention spans. Don't make them dig to find out who you are. Give your portfolio website just enough text, images, and examples to paint an accurate picture. If you can't give your own content a crisp and concise design, why should employers trust you to do it for clients?

Also, don't exaggerate the facts when presenting yourself. Our lives are way too public these days to bother. More important than bragging or dazzling anyone with half-truths is finding a team whose needs and interests align with your own. If you get hired under false pretenses, you will have wasted everyone's time. Even experienced designers with great portfolios aren't the right fit, disposition-wise, for every agency they apply to.

Wolfgang Bartelme: As I mentioned before, I'm a huge fan of the interdisciplinary approach. At most companies, you are unlikely to work exclusively in a single field. In fact, when you do Web design, being able to do some decent-looking icons or cut a simple screencast or promo video is good. This becomes even more important when you are self-employed. Moreover, this variety makes and keeps work interesting . . . at least that's the case for me.

Chris Coyier: Just being a nice person and easy to work with is pretty huge. I think employers look for that during the interview process, at least as best they can in that short time. Someone incredibly stiff or stand-offish is unlikely to win the job over someone who is happy and casual. Design studios, in my experience, are pretty friendly and casual. Other random advice: become really good at one thing. You'll be a lot more valuable as the guy or girl who knows that one thing really well than as a jack of all trades. Being well-rounded is awesome, but having a spike of talent in one particular area will serve you well.

Walter Apai: Social skills are necessary when dealing with potential clients. Designers should know what their clients do and provide them with the best possible service.

I'd encourage all designers to make themselves a one-stop shop for all of their clients' design needs. That would include Web design, copywriting, printing, etc. If you're not an expert in these fields, team up with a few peers so that you can help each other as needed.

Designers should focus on making the entire process easy for clients, but involve clients in some design decisions as well, so that they feel that they are part of the project.

I suggest asking clients a lot of questions and aiming to truly get to the core of their business and what would work for them. The more we understand our clients and their projects, the more successful the projects will be and the better our chances of getting them as repeat clients.

A designer is a human being, too. Become a well-versed designer, understand your medium, get educated, and become a well-rounded person who always aims high.

Set high standards for yourself and your work. The right clients will gravitate to someone who holds themselves to high standards.

What should new freelancers do during the first few months of their business to succeed?

Paul Andrew: You have to have a personal business plan. I really wish I had a plan when I started out; I really do. I jumped right in feet first and landed on my head! And it hurt. Partly, I think it was those first few months of hardship that even now propel me forward. That period not only affected my finances and confidence, it damaged my reputation. That is very hard to regain. I think over the years I have regained it, but it was hard work, and it all could have been avoided with a bit more planning and simply by writing a personal business strategy.

It's not enough to have a strategy planned out in your head; it has to be on paper. You need to be able to read it and see it to live by it. Every so often you should read it again, just to realign yourself. And then read it again, and only tweak it if you really have to.

Your personal business plan could do the following:

- Describe your business objectives, business direction and where you hope to be in x number of months.
- List all potential pitfalls and how to avoid them.
- Set honest and realistic targets, and allow for a little flexibility.
- As your business grows, track its achievements and compare them to your business objectives.

- Set up a financial framework to measure how much your business is making (or not making).
- Describe how you will attract new business to meet your financial targets.

Everyone and every business is different. Write down what is correct and achievable for you, and be very honest: it is your business after all. Stick to the plan!

Brian Hoff: Personally, I worked for nearly three years while preparing to go freelance. I would work my 9:00 to 5:00 job, come home, eat dinner and then market myself (blog), search for new business, advertise, and work from around 7:00 pm until 12:00 am. Having a good feel for running your own business is important before you go in head first.

Saving money is also important. Every business, no matter what it is, goes through periods of drought. Having money to back you up for a little while is a must. Freelancing is not for everyone. Part-time freelancing while maintaining a steady-paying job will help you get a feel for things.

Chris Spooner: I think the most important time in freelancing isn't particularly the first few months, but more so the time leading up to going freelance. As a freelancer, you'll need a good flow of clients to generate income; you'll have to get busy promoting and building a name for yourself, so that when you're ready to leave your job, you'll be all set to simply flick the switch from employment to self-employment.

During this build-up time, you'll want to design all of your personal branding, especially your website, to showcase what you can do. Become an active member of the design community by blogging, guest writing and networking via Twitter (or you might want to network offline or locally), and begin taking on projects that you can work on during the nights. It can be hard work managing both your full-time job and one or two freelance projects simultaneously, but when the number of inquiries reaches an optimal level, you can quickly switch from your job to taking on more freelance work — rather than making the decision one day, falling flat on your face and then having to eat beans on toast until you've built a profile.

Jon Phillips: I believe the first few months are crucial, especially because it usually means quitting the day job and taking the plunge into the freelancing world. It can be scary at first. Many things need to be done in the first few months, but of course nothing is irreparable. Should you make a bad decision, you can always fix things as you go along. I highly recommend getting a portfolio website up; even if you don't have a lot to show, you need a place to showcase what you have. Then get a good invoicing system such as Freshbooks or Billings, network with other freelancers as much as possible via Twitter, Facebook, design forums and blogs, and maybe start a blog of your own.

Elliot Jay Stocks: Work for someone else! For the first few months to be a success, you need to have work lined up, so having that in place before you make the jump is important. I'd also recommend getting a good accountant as soon as you can and some sort of system for keeping track of your money, such as Xero. Also, make sure you have a website set up long before you decide to go solo.

Aside from design and technical skills, what aspects of running a business should new freelancers focus on?

Paul Andrew: The advice I have been given over the years about freelancing as a business has varied. Some have told me that putting business ahead of design guarantees profit and keeps your head above water. On the other hand, I have also been told not to treat design as a business, to work on what your passion is, the business side will take care of itself.

These are both great philosophies, but they don't really work in the real world. The answer is to have a healthy balance between the two. Both need to be kept separate while at the same time working off each other. Think of it as the positive and negative charge of a battery. The battery only works when both charges are connected. (You can decide which is the positive and negative side in relation to business and design.)

When meeting potential clients, first impressions really do count, and you really need to present yourself with professionalism. It does not matter how strong your portfolio is or who you are — it is about how professional and business-like you appear to them. You are negotiating a business transaction after all.

Yes, this means breaking away from the designer stereotype of wearing T-shirts and jeans and instead being clean-shaven, putting on a business suit, and remembering the manners your mother taught you. Carry business cards with you, maybe even a briefcase; do what you have to do to convince the client you mean business.

Some monkeys you should not carry on your back by yourself, and they are the finance side of your business. Let's be honest: who understands tax and monetary law? I certainly don't and don't care to either. Find yourself an accountant. They don't cost that much — maybe a week's wage out of the year, and when you weigh the cost of doing your taxes incorrectly and the penalties that might follow, an accountant is a worthwhile investment.

It would be nice if everyone you worked with was honest. Protecting the integrity of your work, yourself, and your business should be next on your to-do list. The reality is that at some point, someone will try to shortchange you or, worse, wiggle out of a payment. That is why you need a watertight contract. Every country has its own laws regarding design; make sure you know and understand yours.

Hiring a lawyer to write a standard contract for your small business would be expensive. A way around this would be to write your own, as I did. I asked a few designers for advice and researched the law online and came up with an outline for my own. I then took it to a lawyer and asked them to sanity-check it. Not as expensive as asking them to write it — still, it wasn't cheap, but it was worth it.

So, to sum up, if you're dressed smart, your business finances are in safe hands, and you are legally protected, then you are free to do what you were trained to do and give your creativity free rein, letting your passion fuel your design. It is a long road to take, but it is necessary.

Brian Hoff: Marketing without a doubt. I receive many emails asking how I get so much freelance business or how I find clients. My response: you have to work hard for it. Clients won't come to you. Tell everyone what you do, start a blog, attend networking events and conferences, contact clients directly. Running your own business is hard work. There is no such thing as a 40-hour work week when you run your own business. I work seven days a week. I've even gone so far as to strike up new work by chatting with someone at the bar (not recommended). You have to have personality and drive to freelance successfully.

Jon Phillips: Being a freelancer means having to wear many different hats (a ton of different hats!). Spending some time on government websites and meeting with an accountant to learn more about tax laws goes a very long way. Of course, many designers, being creative types, tend to forget that it's a business (I often forget). You need to spend time on accounting but also on networking and marketing your business. In the first few months results will be small, but your efforts will pay off in the long run. You need to be as good with numbers as you are with Photoshop.

What are some of the best ways for new designers to find clients?

Henry Jones: I can only speak from experience here. Shortly before I went full-time freelancing, my portfolio was listed on several popular CSS galleries. From that point on, clients found me. I was very surprised to see how many people used the galleries to find designers. Once I had a few clients and projects under my belt, I started to get a lot of referrals. So, work hard on creating a great portfolio, and use the design galleries. This is probably the best and easiest way to get the most exposure. Plenty of design-specific job boards are available where you can search for projects that are a good fit for you.

Jon Phillips: I think websites such as Twitter are a great place to get started! In fact, I found a lot of my own clients via Twitter. Design forums are also a great place to network, make friends and find work. New freelancers may also be tempted to try design contests and crowd-sourcing, but I personally think they devalue the industry, so I wouldn't advise doing that. Even if you don't have much to show in your portfolio, there are others ways to get gigs. There are always job boards, such as the one on Smashing Magazine and the one on FreelanceSwitch, which are great for finding clients. You might even consider buying banner ads on design-related websites. But your marketing budget may not allow this at first, so networking websites, job boards, and forums would be the places to hang out.

Jacob Cass: Get your name out there. Start blogging. Showcase your work. Look on job boards. Ask friends, family, local charities. Read books and blog posts. The information is out there. Your job is to find it!

Walter Apai: Networking is one of the best ways but often one of the most overlooked. I suggest that new designers speak to everyone they know and use every chance they have to talk about their work and what they do for a living.

I found myself just mentioning Web design to someone the other day (not even looking for more work), and immediately they thought of someone they knew who was looking for a website redesign. Opportunities are everywhere; just seize them.

I should also mention that one should not rely on networking alone or any other single "system." I'd encourage new designers to take a multi-faceted approach to their new career.

There are unlimited ways to get new clients. Posting on bulletin boards, both online and offline, and placing small ads in the newspaper or local magazines are just a few of the media you can use. I also think that starting local is best, and getting experience working on projects with people who you can meet in person in your own city. This is a good starting point to gain more "field" experience.

Paul Boag: It has to start with friends and family. This will help build your initial portfolio. From there, consider doing some discounted work for a local charity to gain experience in working for real clients. After that, the contacts you have made through networking will start to pay off, and hopefully you will get some work through them. Finally and most importantly, make it known that you want work. It is surprising how many freelance websites I visit that don't state whether they currently accept work or not.

That said, I would suggest that if you are straight out of university, you should probably work for a small agency before jumping into the freelance world. Being a freelancer requires a lot of business skills that they don't teach you in university.

What networking tips do you have for young designers?

Henry Jones: One option is to attend design conferences, but for young designers this can be expensive. So, I would recommend getting involved in the design community. Start reading and leaving comments on popular design blogs. Create a Twitter account, and post useful stuff. Depending on how much time you have, you could even start your own design-related blog. Blogging has been huge for me, and I believe it's the best way to get your name out there and meet other designers. No matter what route you take, just remember to be helpful and genuine, and you will build lasting relationships.

Paul Andrew: You are young — you cannot change that fact — and you want to be successful. In any business, especially ours, you need friends, you need contacts, and most importantly you need to build professional relationships. Bear in mind, though, that networking is not something you can rush; it takes time and patience.

The best time to start networking is right now. Even if you are still in high school or haven't yet graduated college, reach out now. It is never too early to get your name out there. Your name is your most powerful and memorable asset. Work will follow, I promise.

149

The most important relationships for any designer are the ones they have built with fellow students. No matter what happens, they are your primary network. You can help each other by sharing knowledge and design contacts and by learning from each other.

The best way to network beyond your inner circle is to get in touch with seasoned designers. For the most part, designers are pretty selfless and love to share and help when they can. With that in mind, put together a list of designers on whom you want to model yourself and someone with a strong body of work. Send them emails, accompanied by your portfolio, stating that you are a young designer starting out and seeking a little advice. Ask them how they got started, and ask for any tips they might be willing to share. Seasoned designers need to build their networks, too, and will welcome your introduction and questions.

When I started out as a designer, I sent a letter (with my portfolio and business card) to a local design agency — certainly not the biggest one or the most prestigious — and introduced myself as a young designer who was eager to learn. I asked if I could come in for a day or two to learn a bit about the design business and gain some work experience. Thankfully, they consented, and I spent three days asking questions, picking up business cards, and meeting clients. That was over ten years ago, and I still rely on those contacts. And to this day, that has been my most productive and successful period of networking.

Not every design agency will be as open as that one was, but I would try. There is no harm in asking.

One thing to remember about networking is that success is determined not by your number of contacts but by the quality of those contacts. Even if the best designer in the world sent you a courtesy email reply, it does not mean that you are in their network or that they are in yours. A quality network contact is someone who gives you a personal reply and genuinely tries to help you. These are the contacts you must maintain. This is your network.

Finally, please don't think of youth as an impediment. Think of it as a license to ask questions, to learn, and to expand your personal network.

Paul Boag: Step away from the computer. Meeting people online is great, but nothing beats meeting them face to face. Attend conferences and meet-ups and get to know people. Then follow up on those relationships via Twitter and Facebook.

Also, don't have an agenda. Or, if you have one, be honest and open about it. Too many people network solely to win work or become a "Web celebrity." Instead, network because you want to meet like-minded people who will inspire and excite you about your work.

Soh Tanaka: Attend industry events, seminars, and any kind of social gatherings. Don't be shy; get to know the people around you. Be interested and willing to learn from them, and at the right time let them know who you are and what you do. Carry business cards with you at all times, and have your elevator speech ready. You never know when you will run into a potential client or employer. Networking is all about expanding your opportunities, and as a designer this skill is critical.

Steven Snell has been designing websites for several years. He actively maintains a few blogs of his own, including DesignM.ag, which regularly provides articles and resources for web designers.

Index